# Cursive Handwriting Workbook

# Learn Your Third Grader to Write

## Ages 8-9

This Book
belongs to:

_________________________

_________________________

# Let's remember and practice cursive letters A-Z

These worksheets are a quick reminder on tricky letters

# Cursive A

Trace the cursive letters, then write your own.

Trace the sentence written in script.

# Cursive B

Trace the cursive letters, then write your own.

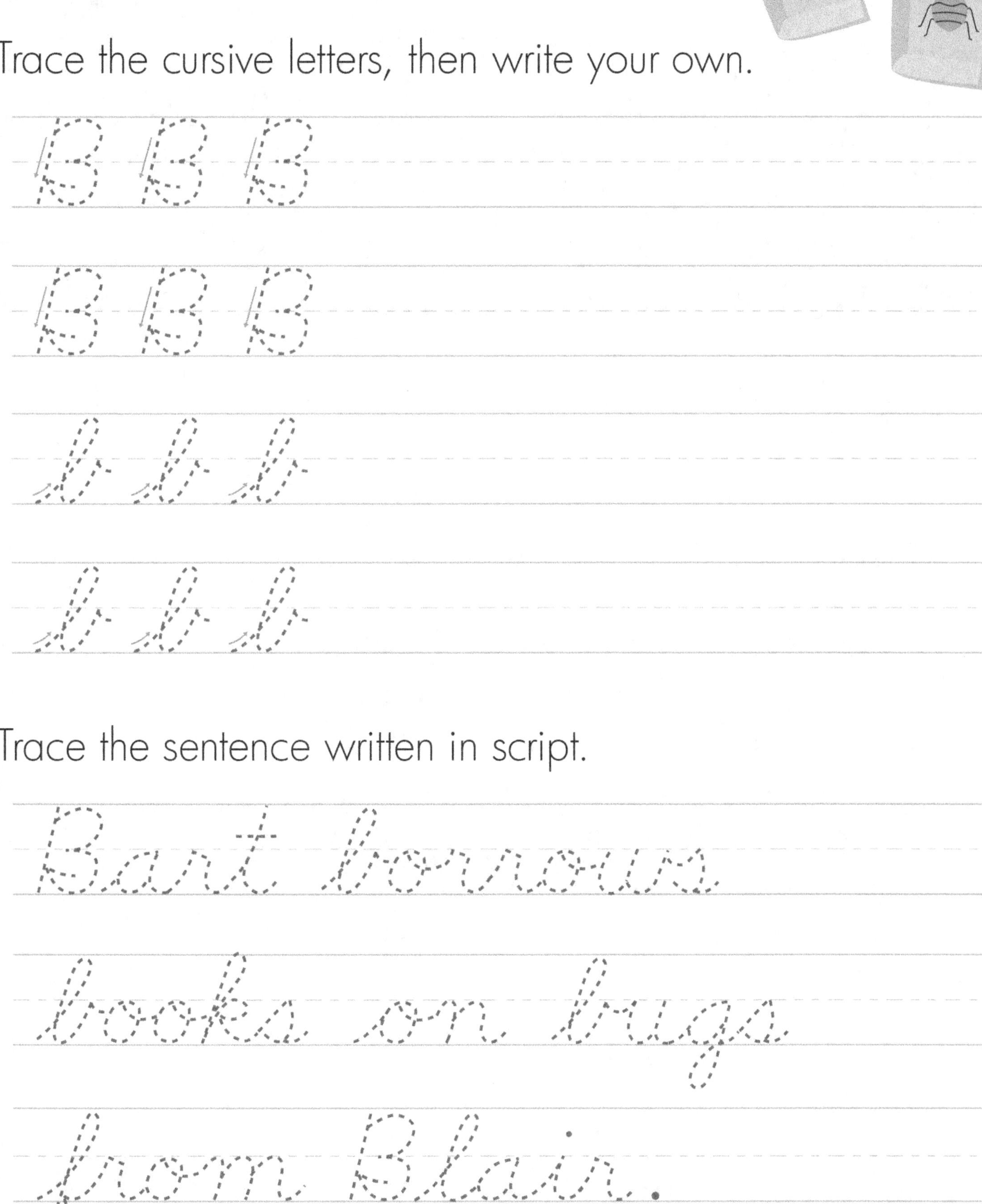

Trace the sentence written in script.

# Cursive C

Trace the cursive letters, then write your own.

Trace the sentence written in script.

# Cursive D

Trace the cursive letters, then write your own.

Trace the sentence written in script.

# Cursive E

Trace the cursive letters, then write your own.

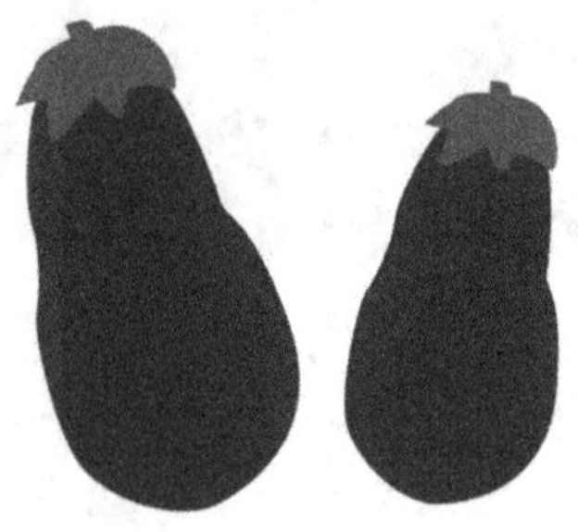

Trace the sentence written in script.

# Cursive F

Trace the cursive letters, then write your own.

F F F

F F F

f f f

f f f

Trace the sentence written in script.

Fred finished first in the frog race.

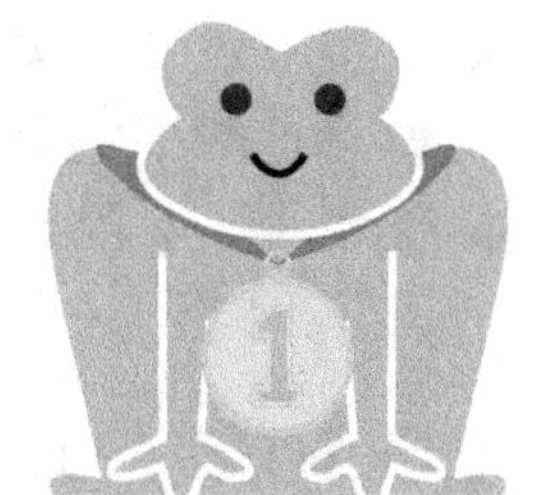

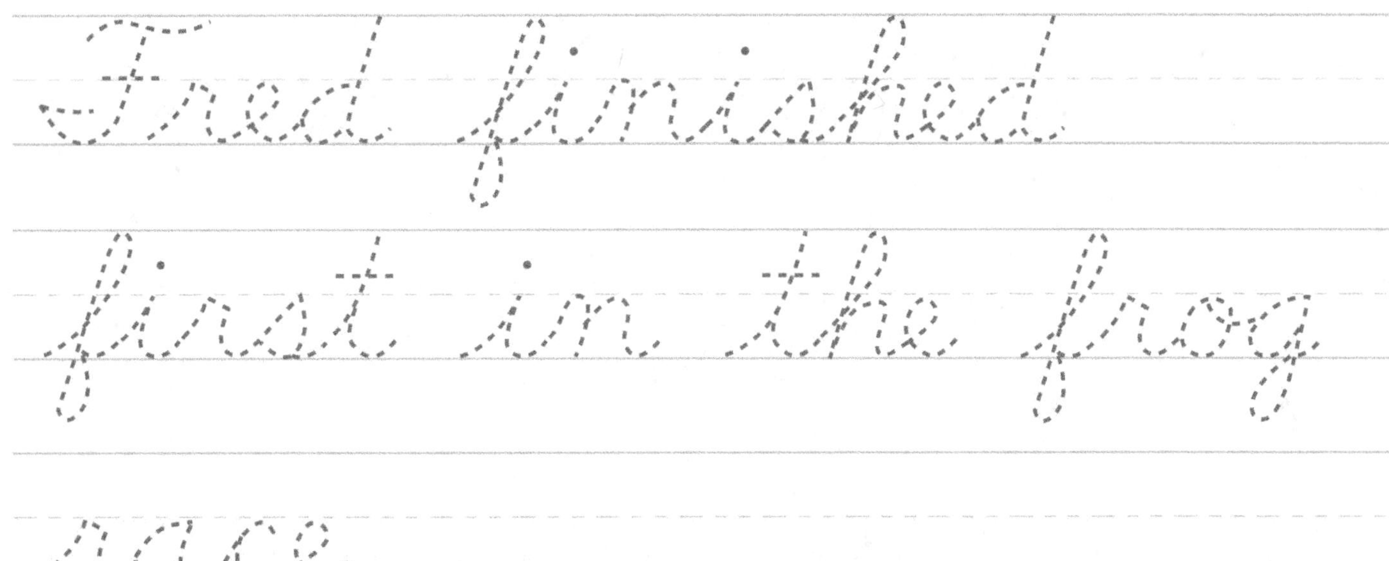

# Cursive G

Trace the cursive letters, then write your own.

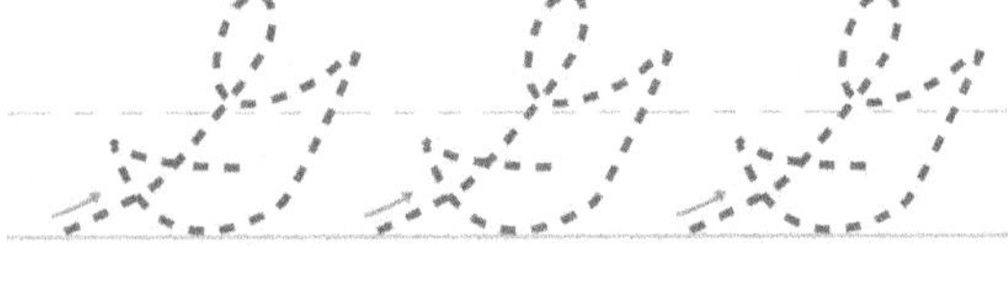

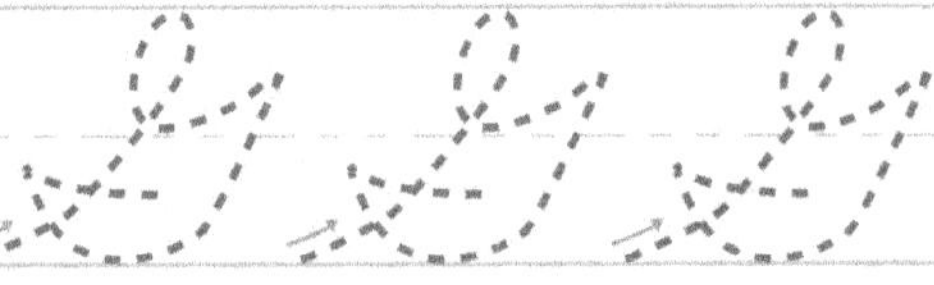

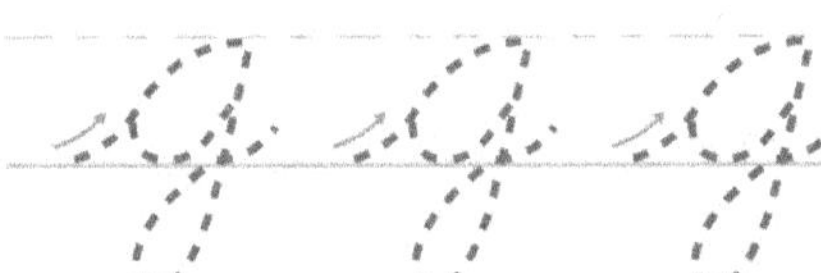

Trace the sentence written in script.

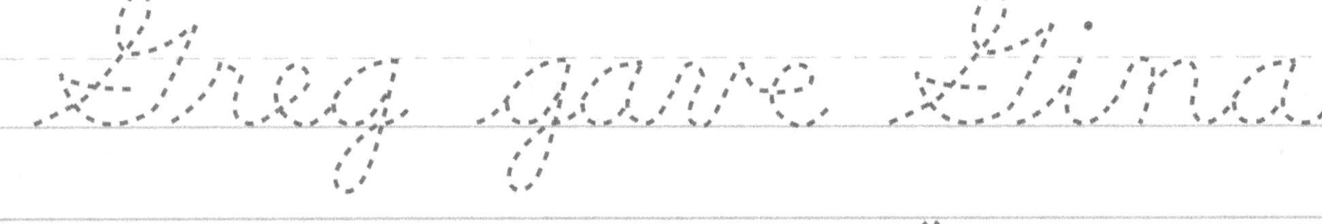


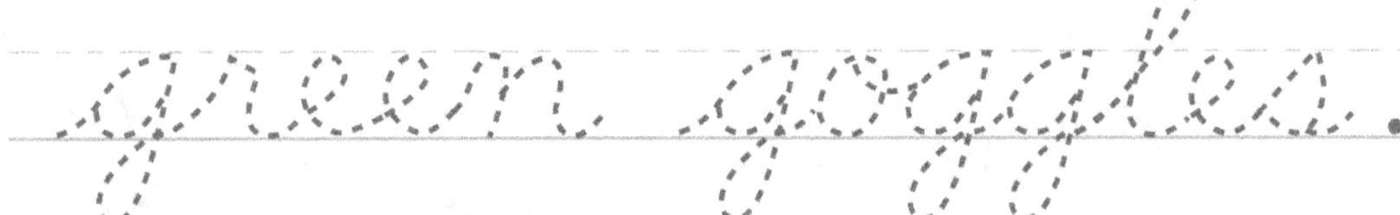

# Cursive H

Trace the cursive letters, then write your own.

H H H

H H H

h h h

h h h

Trace the sentence written in script.

Harry has a
hairy hamster
named Herb.

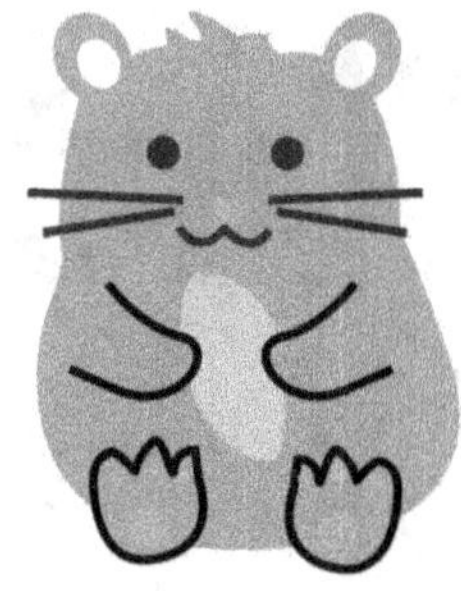

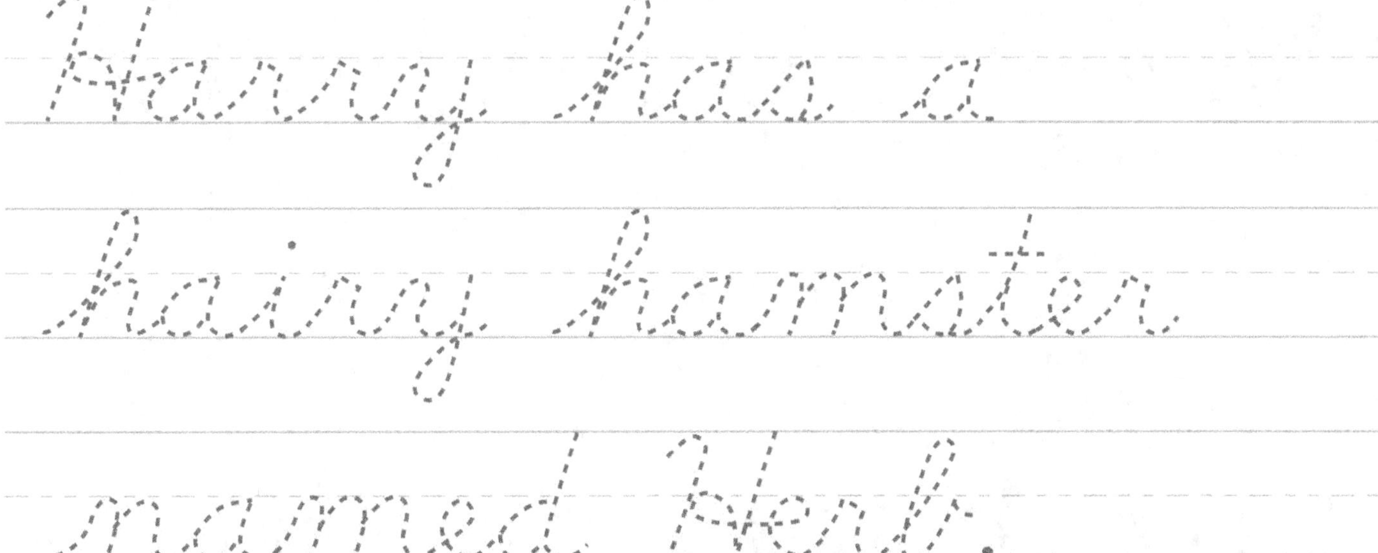

# Cursive I

Trace the cursive letters, then write your own.

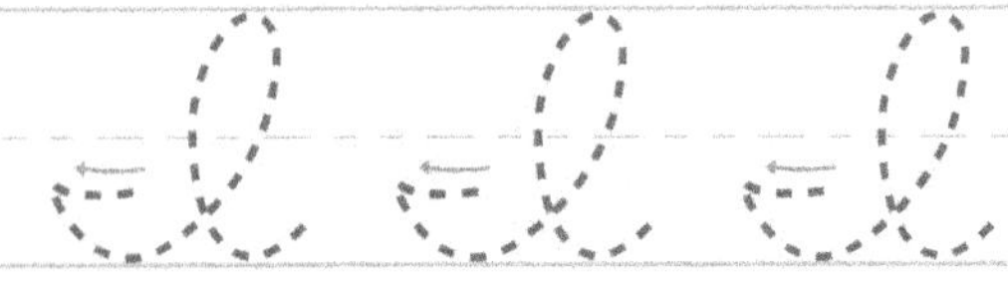

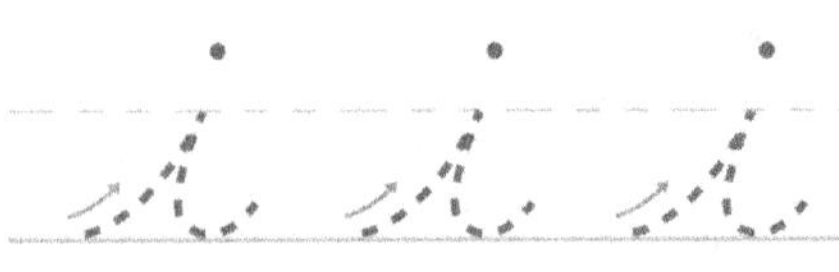

Trace the sentence written in script.

# Cursive J

Trace the cursive letters, then write your own.

J J J

J J J

j j j

j j j

Trace the sentence written in script.

Jenny just ate

jelly from a jar.

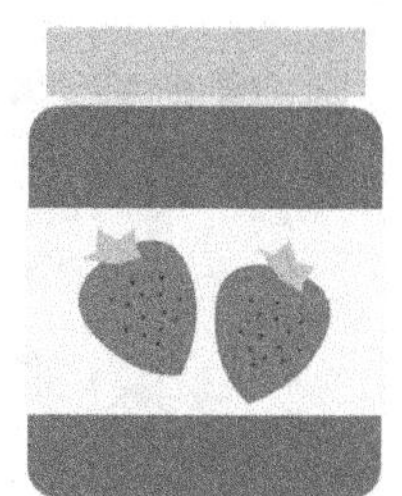

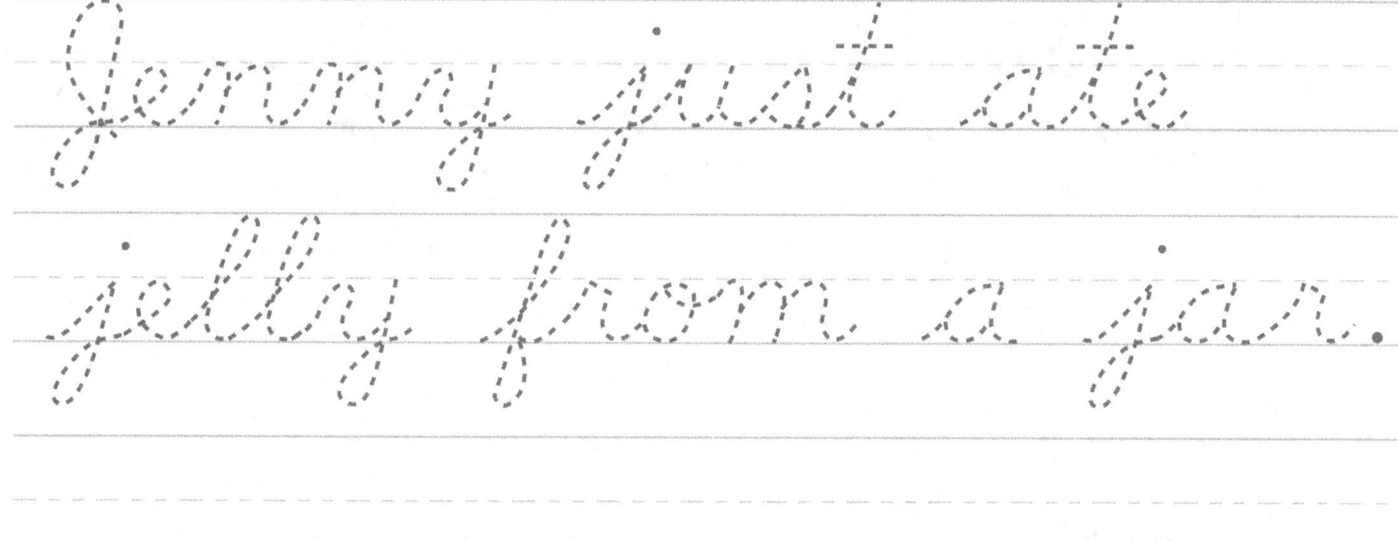

# Cursive K

Trace the cursive letters, then write your own.

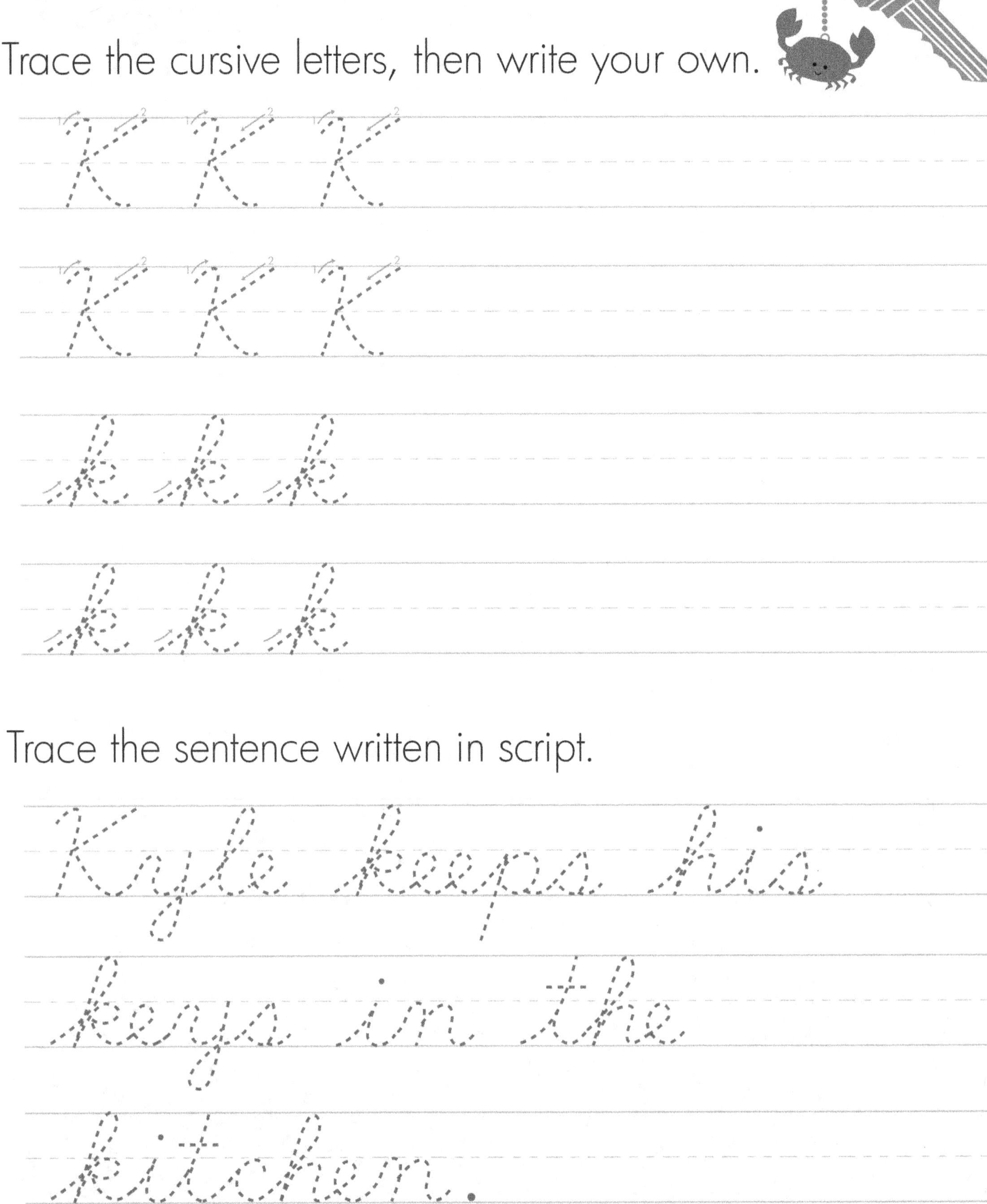

Trace the sentence written in script.

# Cursive L

Trace the cursive letters, then write your own.

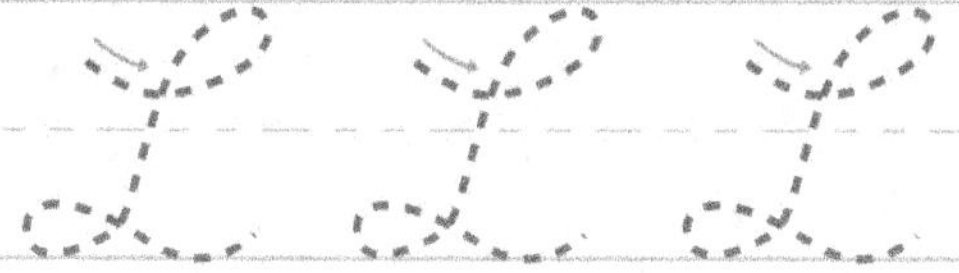

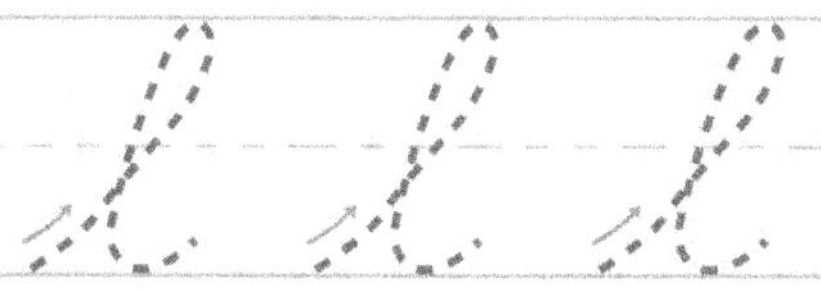

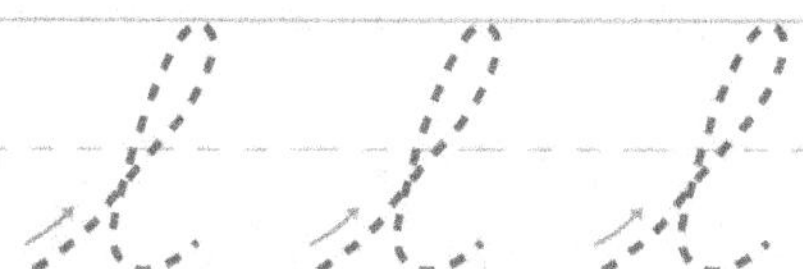

Trace the sentence written in script.

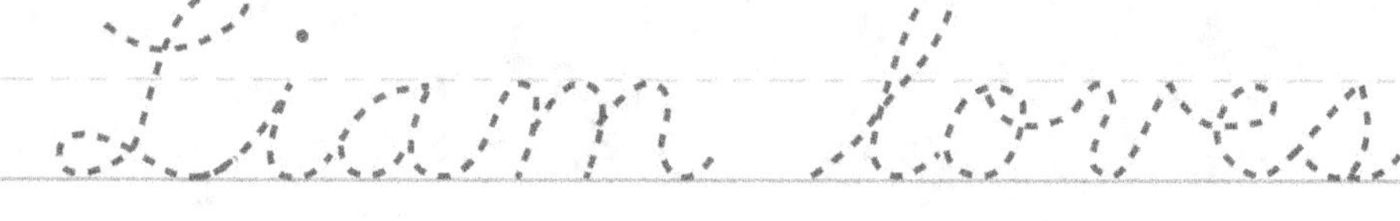


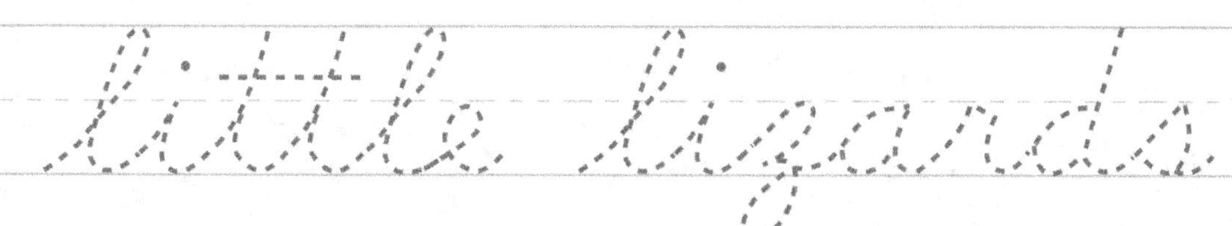


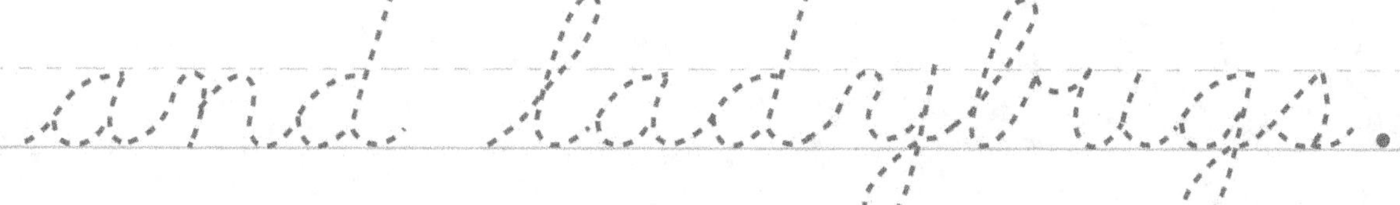

# Cursive M

Trace the cursive letters, then write your own.

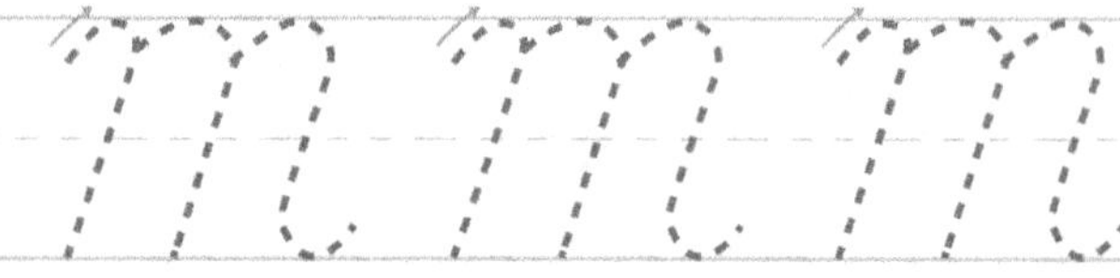

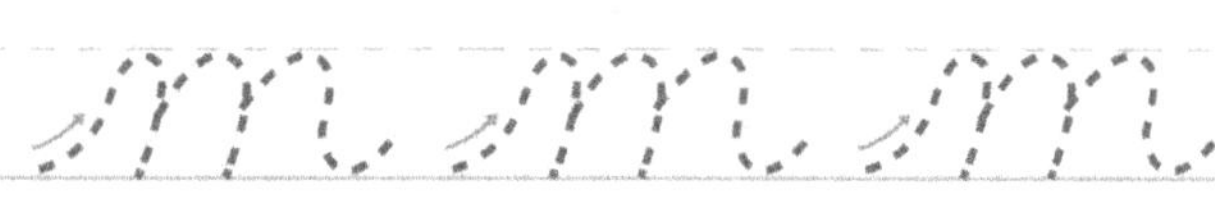

Trace the sentence written in script.

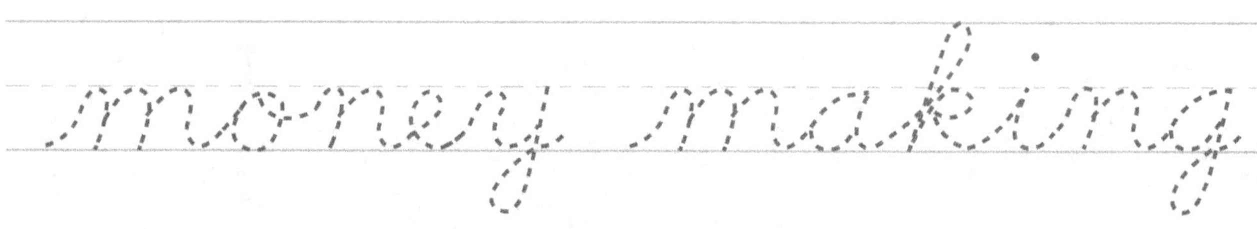

# Cursive N

Trace the cursive letters, then write your own.

Trace the sentence written in script.

# Cursive O

Trace the cursive letters, then write your own.

Trace the sentence written in script.

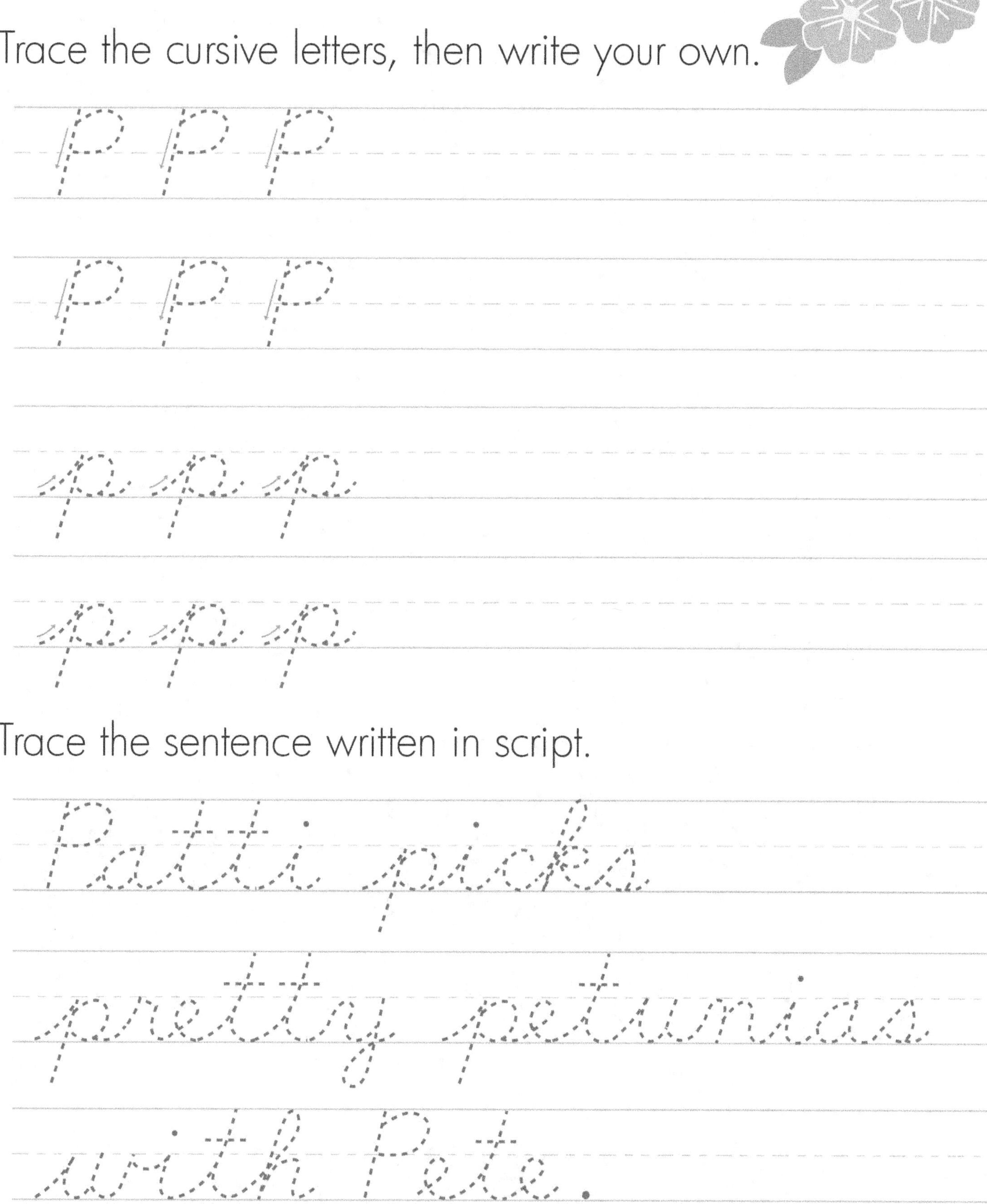

# Cursive P

Trace the cursive letters, then write your own.

Trace the sentence written in script.

# Cursive Q

Trace the cursive letters, then write your own.

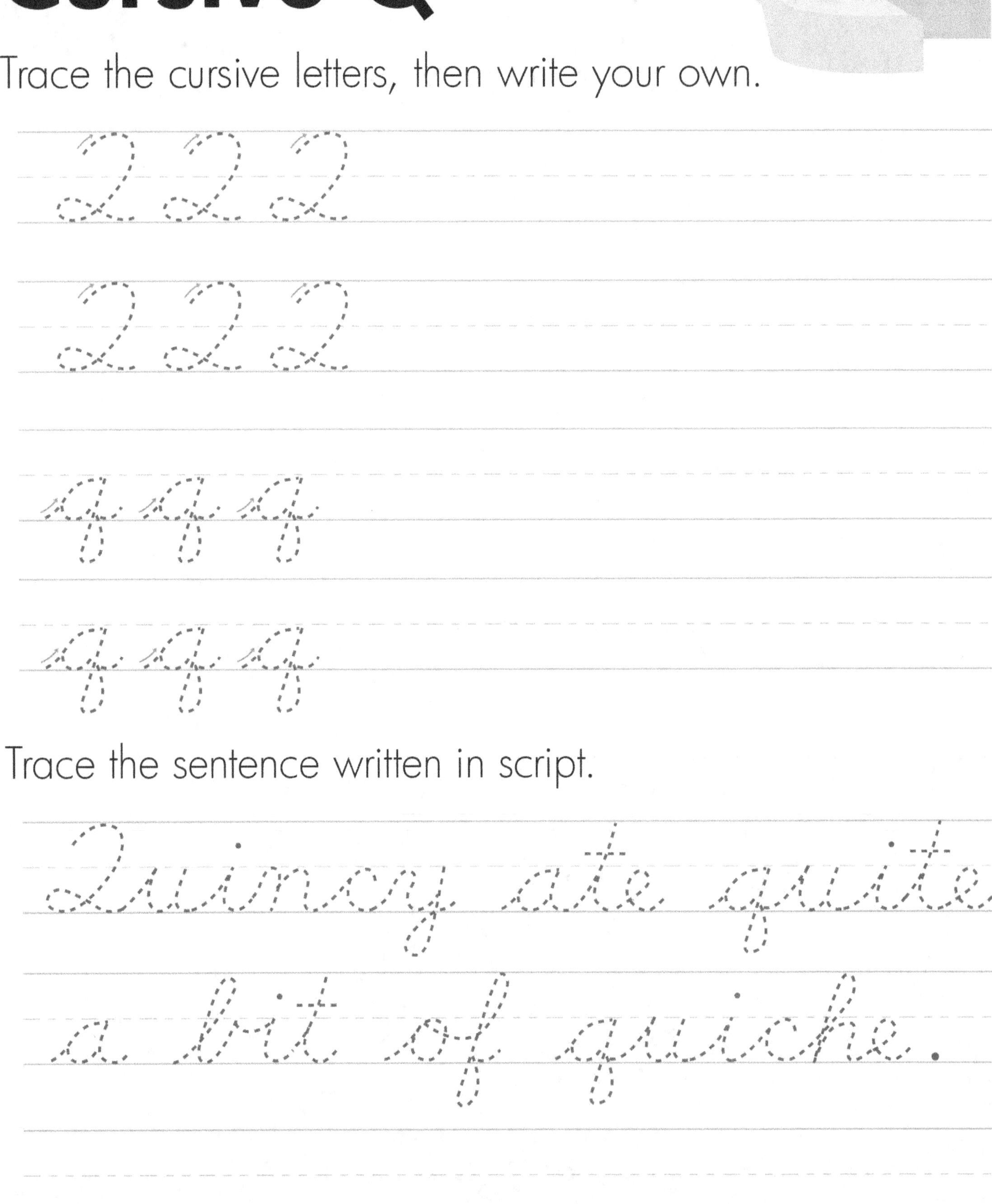

Trace the sentence written in script.

# Cursive R

Trace the cursive letters, then write your own.

Trace the sentence written in script.

# Cursive S

Trace the cursive letters, then write your own.

Trace the sentence written in script.

Samantha sails
on the sea every
Saturday.

# Cursive T

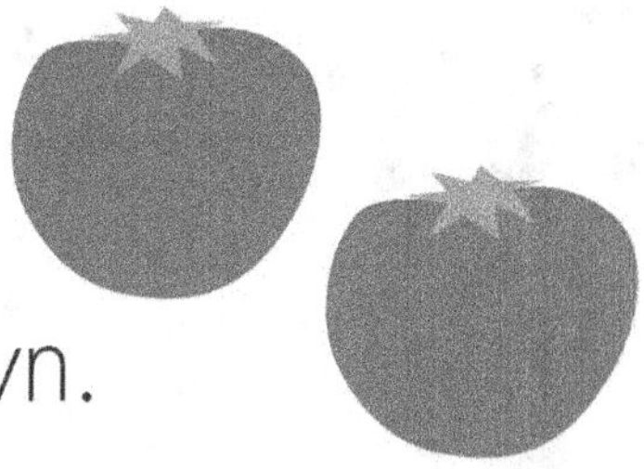

Trace the cursive letters, then write your own.

T T T

T T T

t t t

t t t

Trace the sentence written in script.

Tommy tends to
his tomatoes
every Thursday.

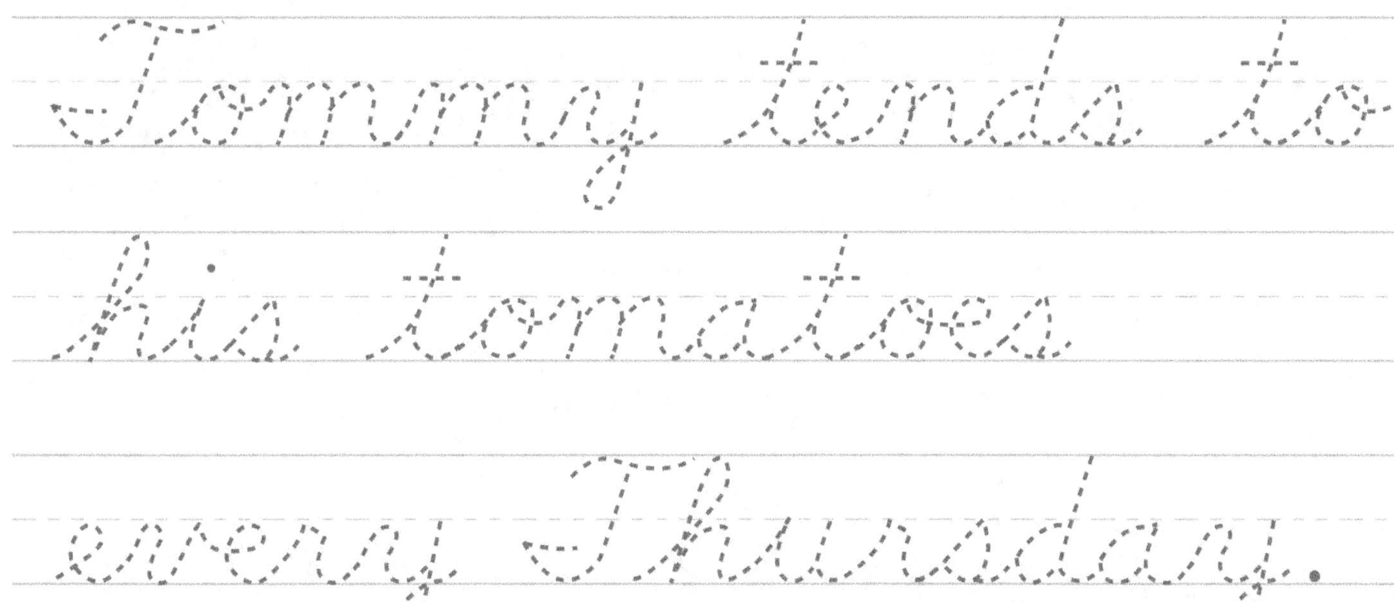

# Cursive U

Trace the cursive letters, then write your own.

Trace the sentence written in script.

# Cursive V

Trace the cursive letters, then write your own.

Trace the sentence written in script.

# Cursive W

Trace the cursive letters, then write your own.

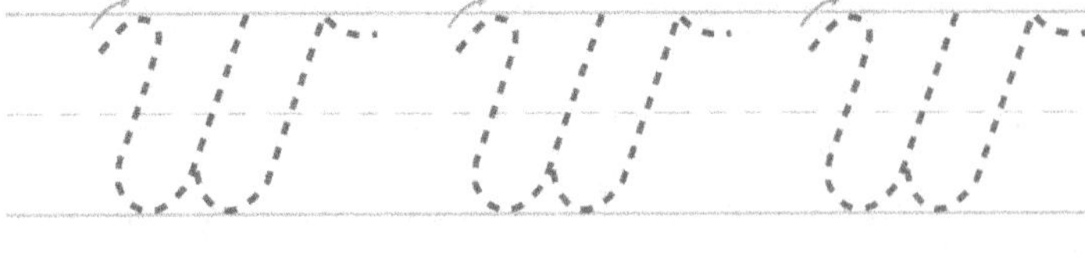

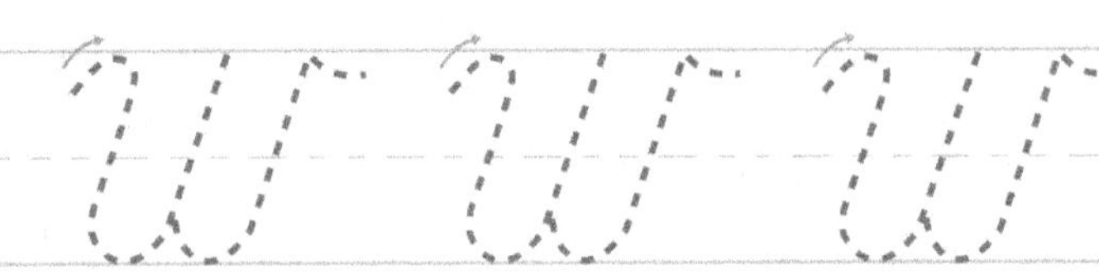

Trace the sentence written in script.

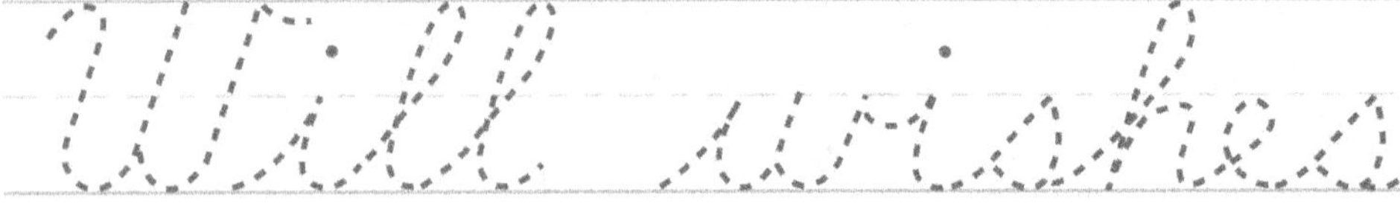


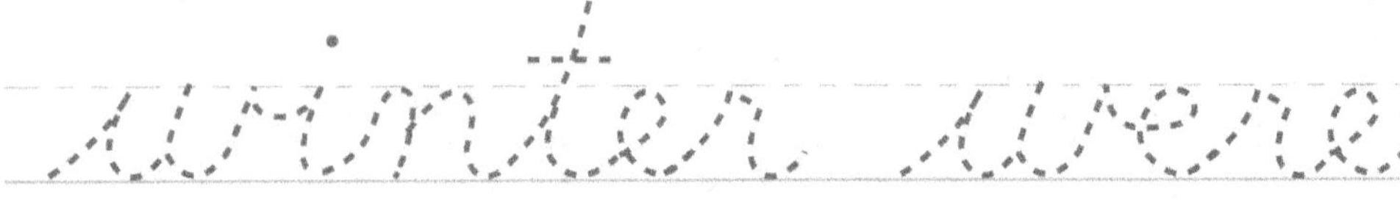

# Cursive X

Trace the cursive letters, then write your own.

Trace the sentence written in script.

Xander took
some excellent
X-rays.

# Cursive Y

Trace the cursive letters, then write your own.

Trace the sentence written in script.

# Cursive Z

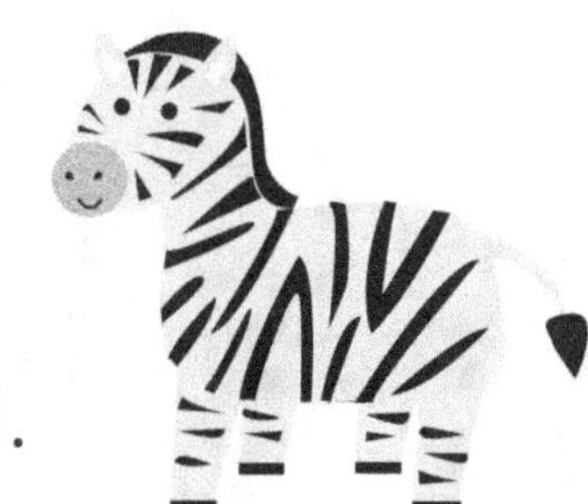

Trace the cursive letters, then write your own.

Z Z Z

Z Z Z

z z z

z z z

Trace the sentence written in script.

Zach zoomed off
to the zoo to see
the zebras.

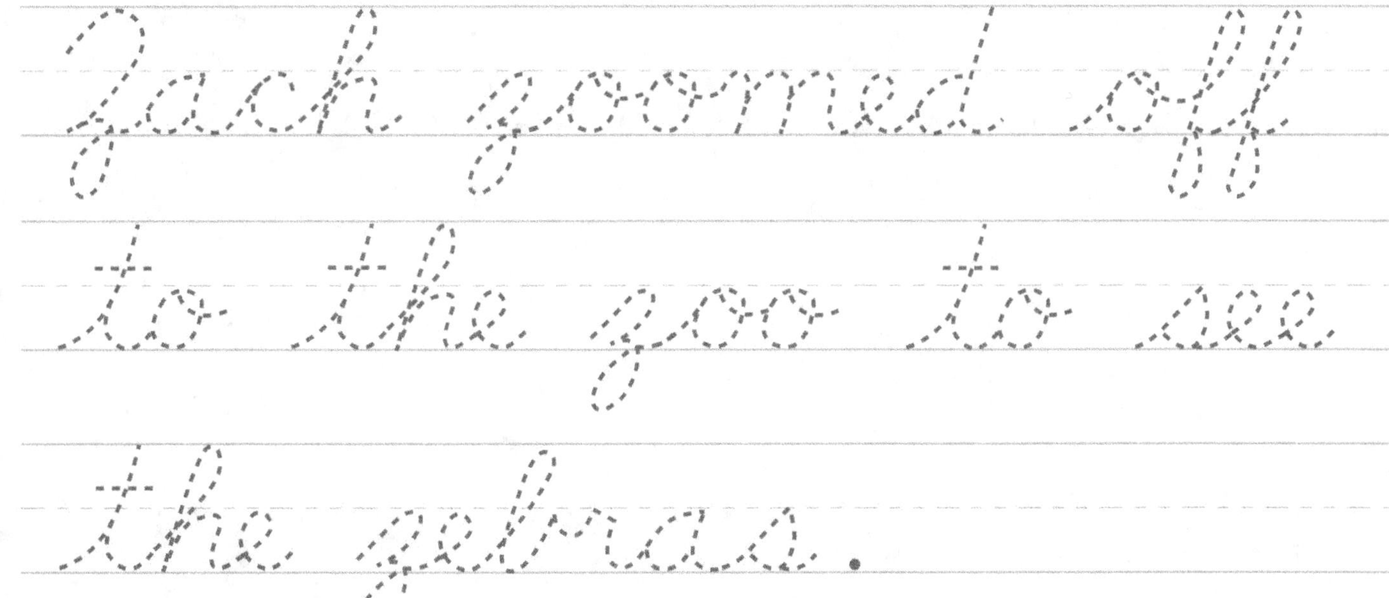

# A is for Alligator

Trace the cursive letters, then write your own.

Trace the sentence written in script, then write your own.

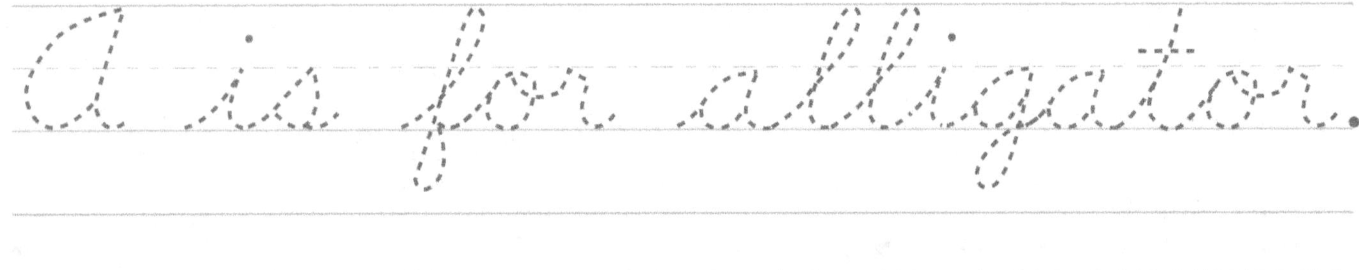

# B is for Bear

Trace the cursive letters, then write your own.

Trace the sentence written in script, then write your own.

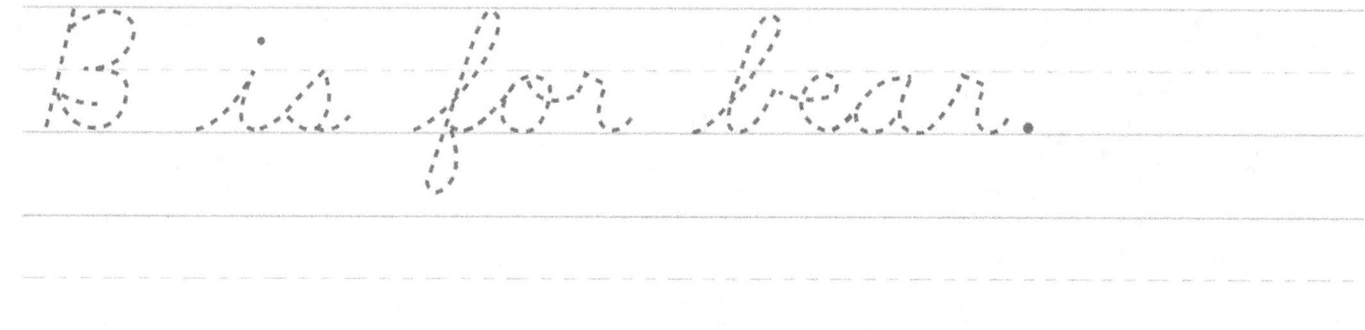

# C is for Caterpillar

Trace the cursive letters, then write your own.

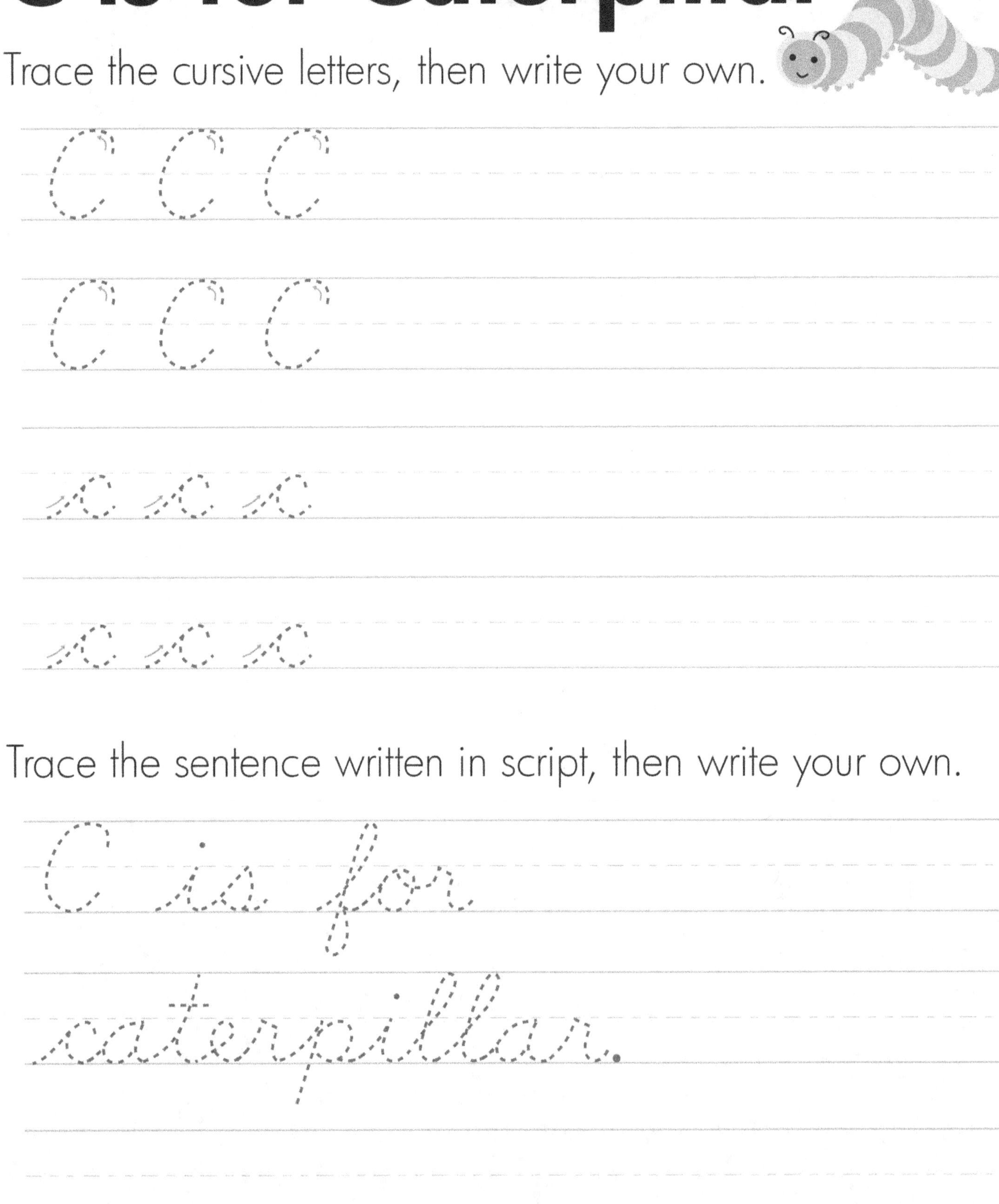

Trace the sentence written in script, then write your own.

# D is for Duck

Trace the cursive letters, then write your own.

Trace the sentence written in script, then write your own.

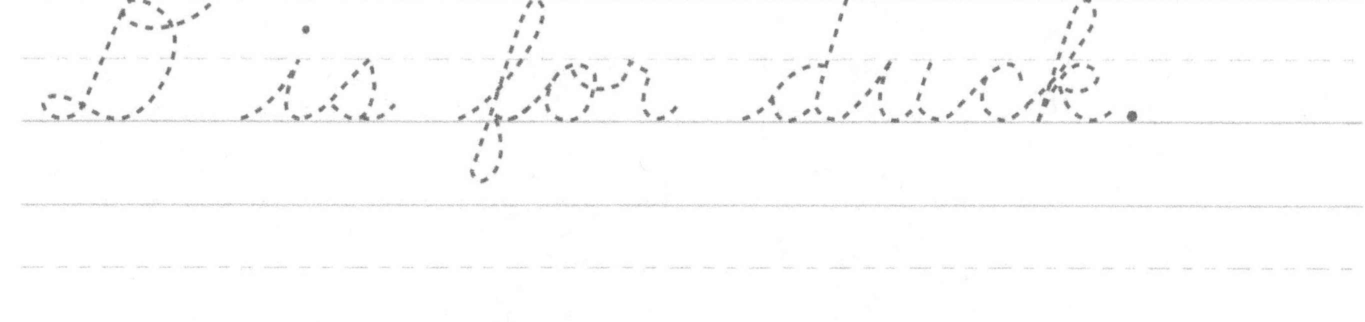

# E is for Elephant

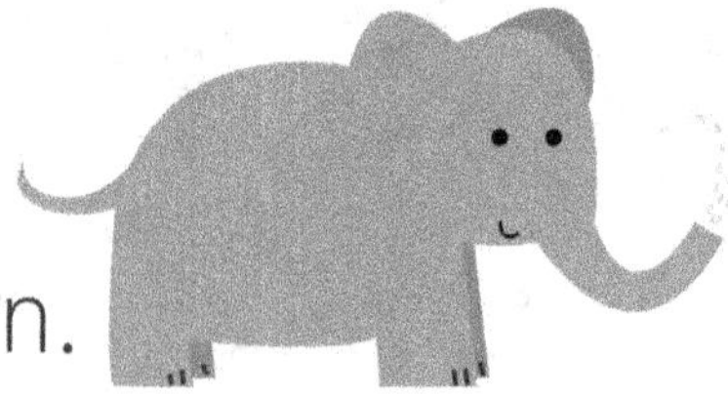

Trace the cursive letters, then write your own.

E E E

E E E

e e e

e e e

Trace the sentence written in script, then write your own.

E is for elephant.

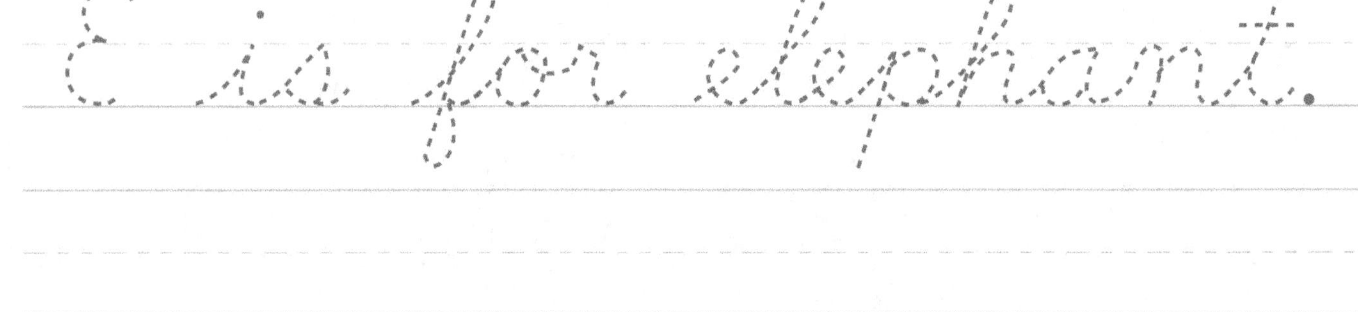

# F is for Fox

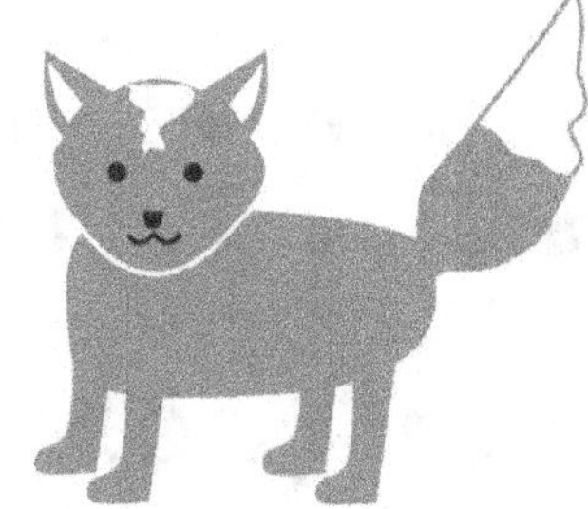

Trace the cursive letters, then write your own.

F F F

F F F

f f f

f f f

Trace the sentence written in script, then write your own.

F is for fox.

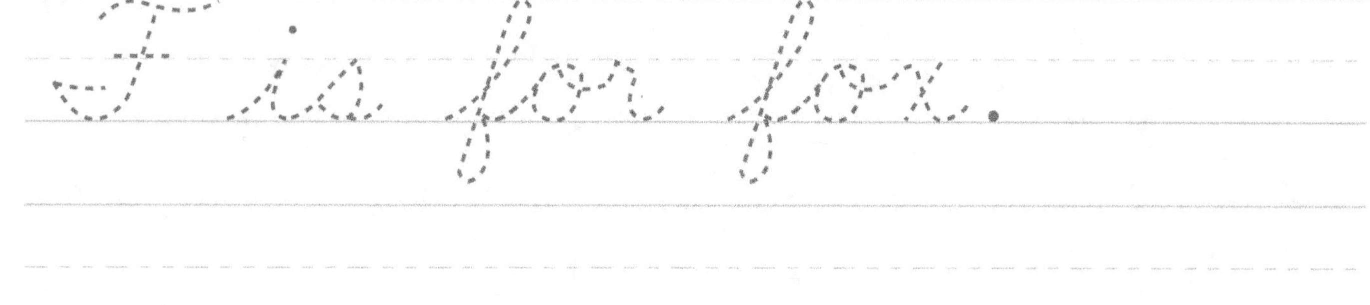

# G is for Giraffe

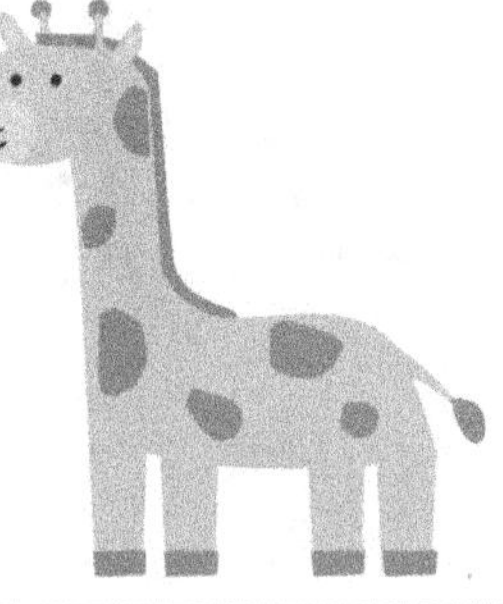

Trace the cursive letters, then write your own.

G G G

G G G

g g g

g g g

Trace the sentence written in script, then write your own.

G is for giraffe.

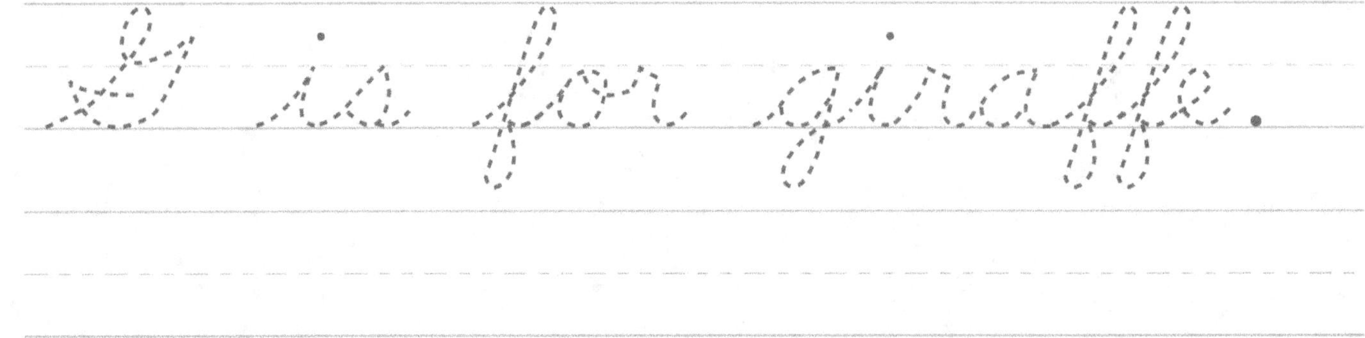

# H is for Hen

Trace the cursive letters, then write your own.

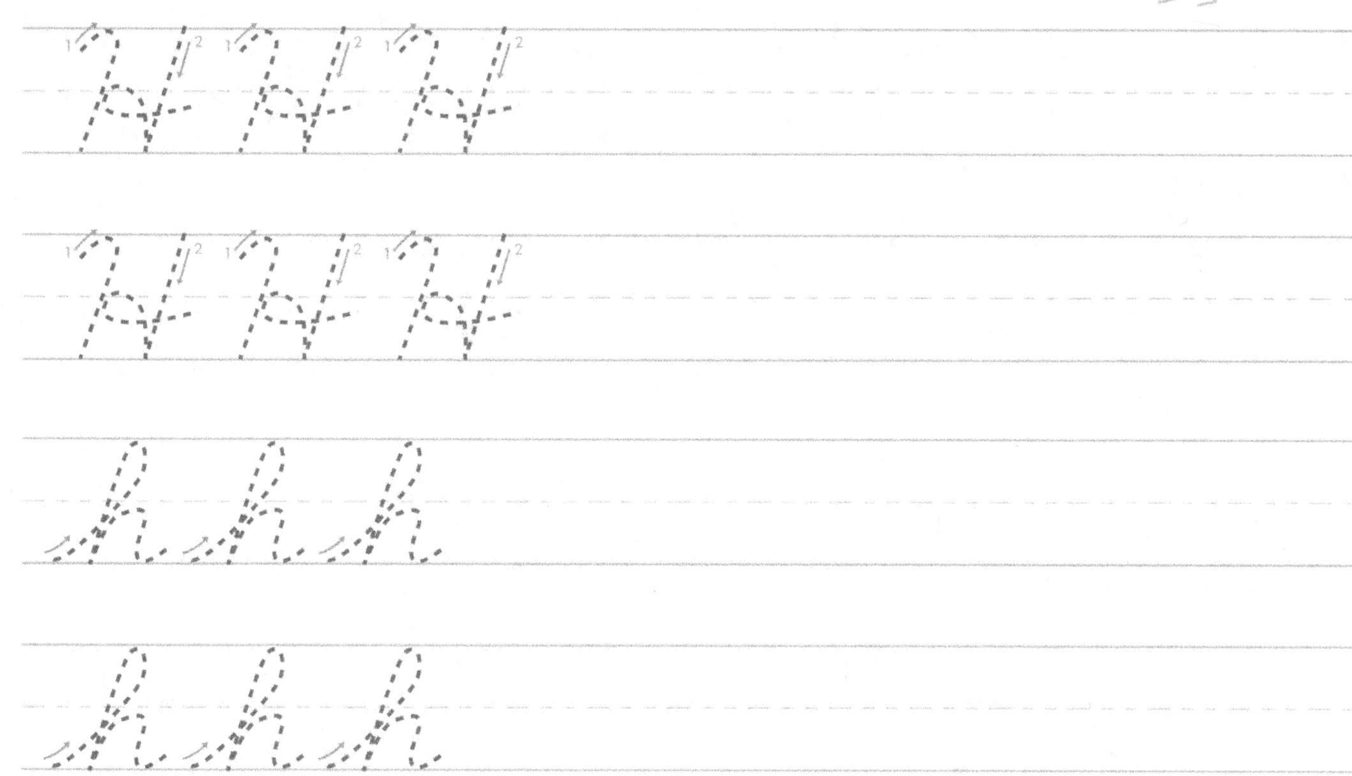

Trace the sentence written in script, then write your own.

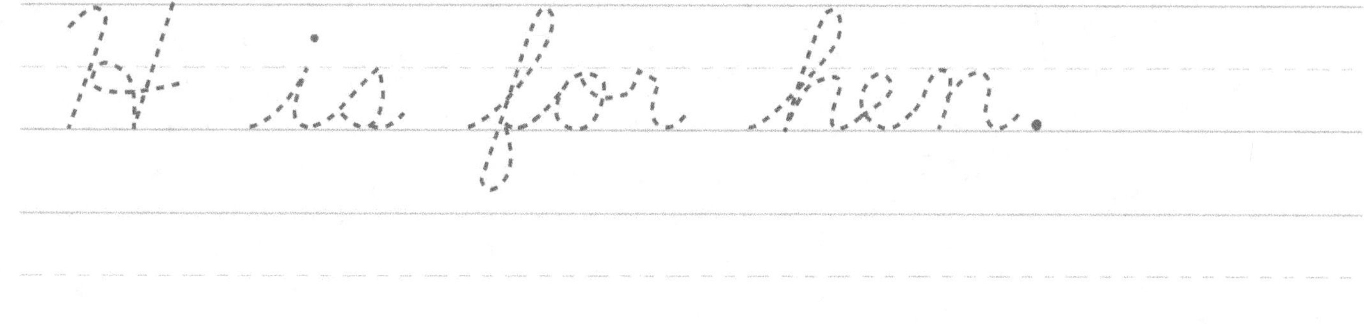

# I is for Iguana

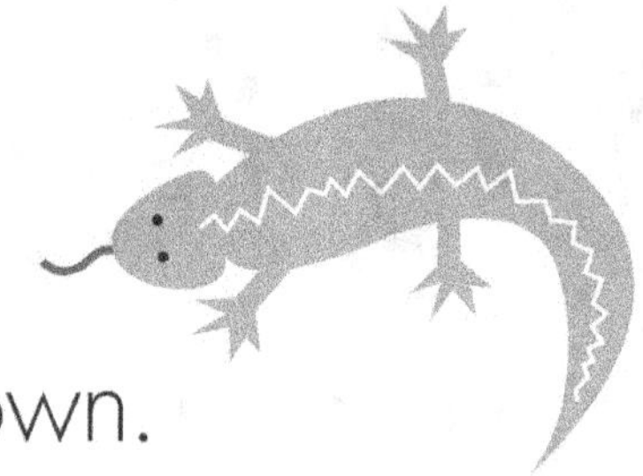

Trace the cursive letters, then write your own.

I I I

I I I

i i i

i i i

Trace the sentence written in script, then write your own.

I is for iguana.

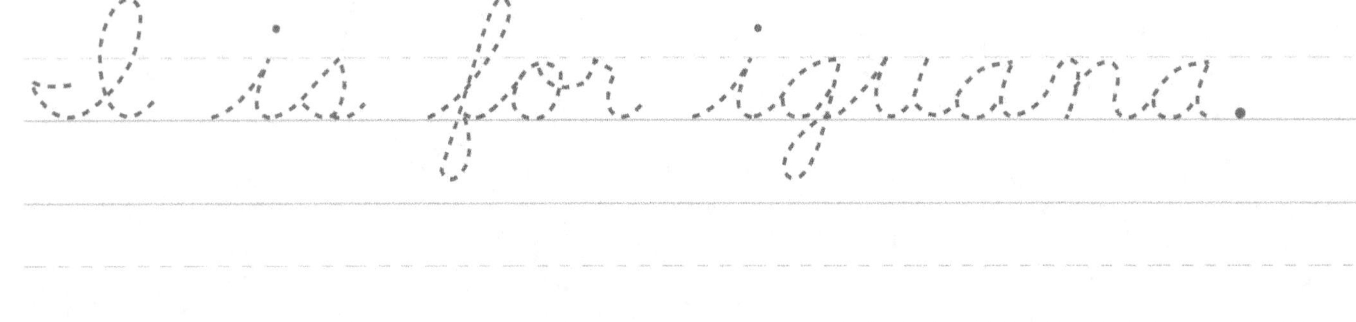

# J is for Jellyfish

Trace the cursive letters, then write your own.

Trace the sentence written in script, then write your own.

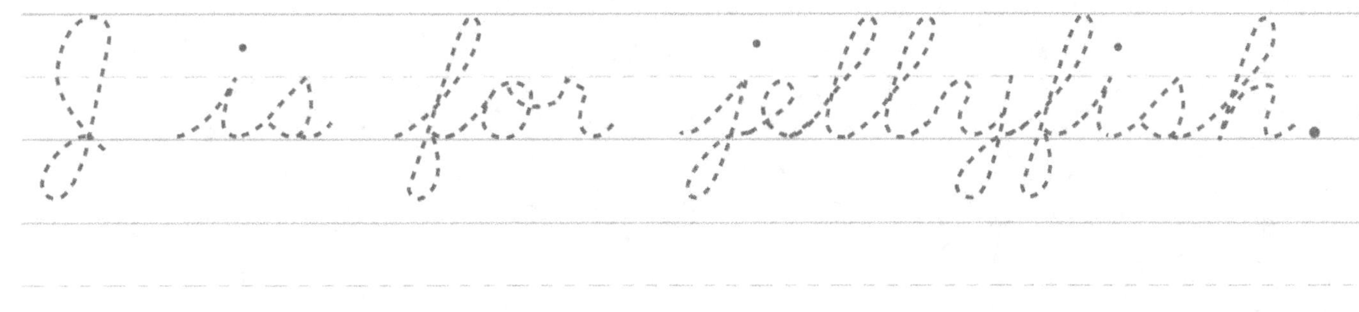

# K is for Koala

Trace the cursive letters, then write your own.

Trace the sentence written in script, then write your own.

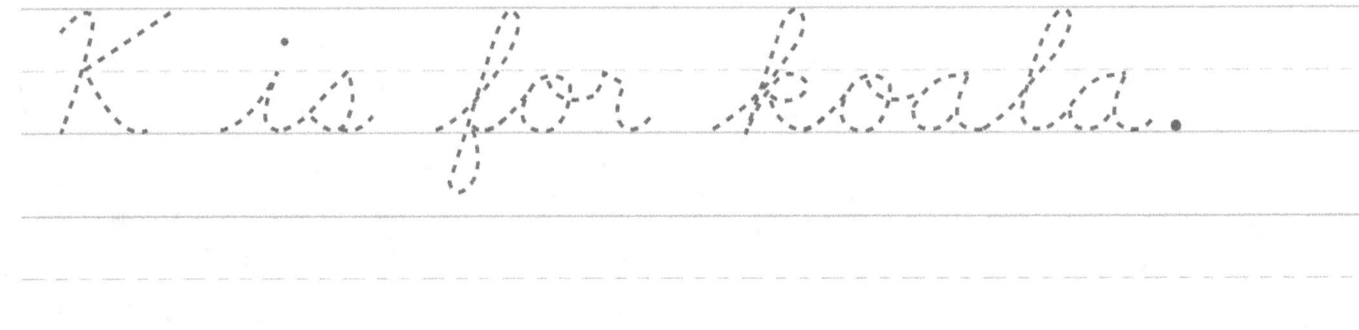

# L is for Llama

Trace the cursive letters, then write your own.

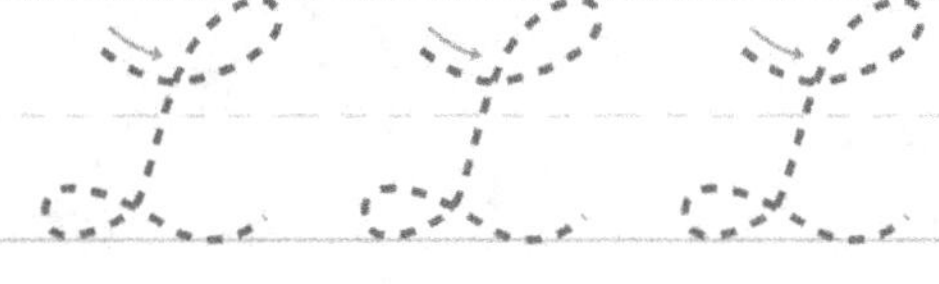

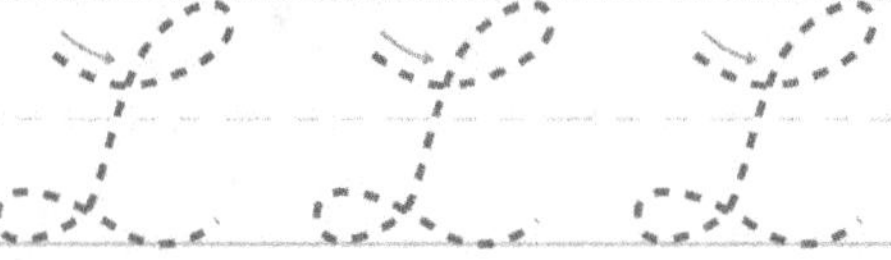

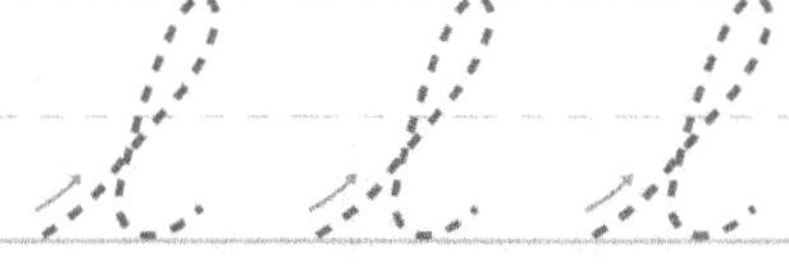

Trace the sentence written in script, then write your own.

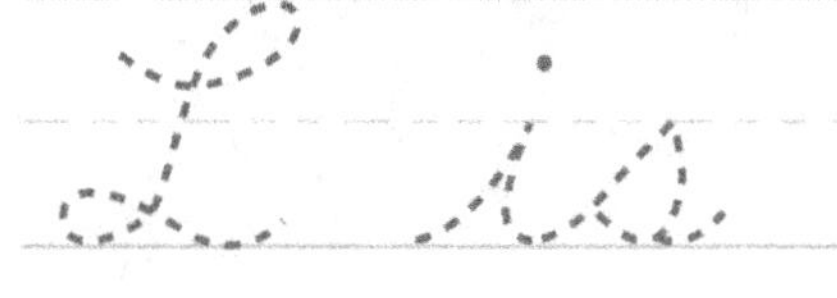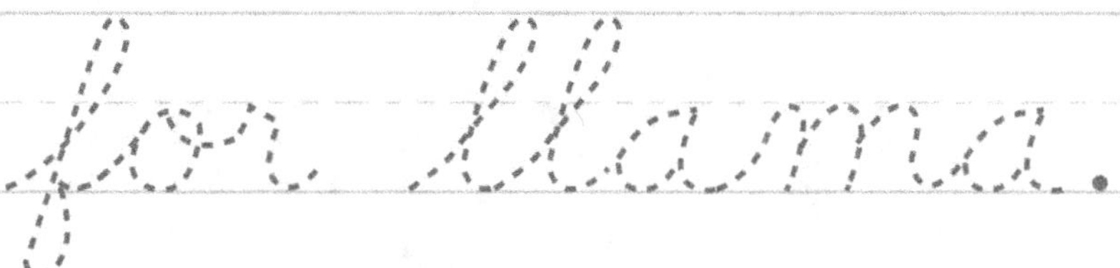

# M is for Monkey

Trace the cursive letters, then write your own.

Trace the sentence written in script, then write your own.

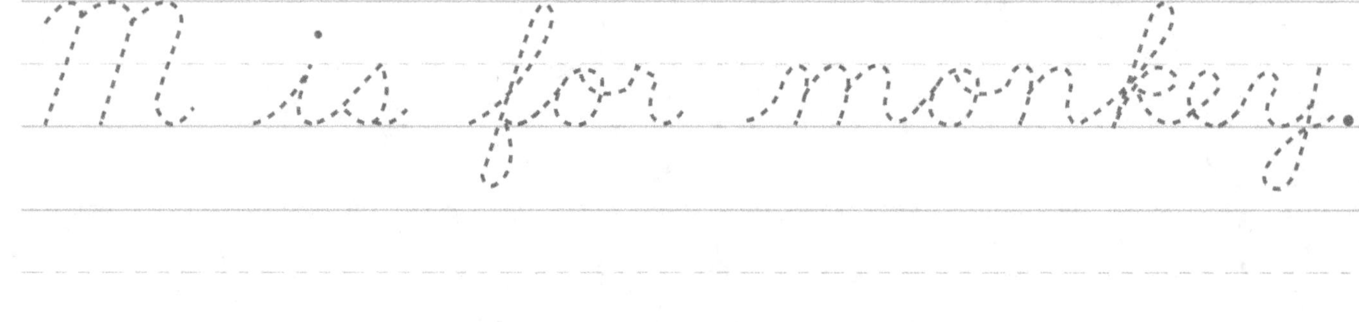

# N is for Narwhal

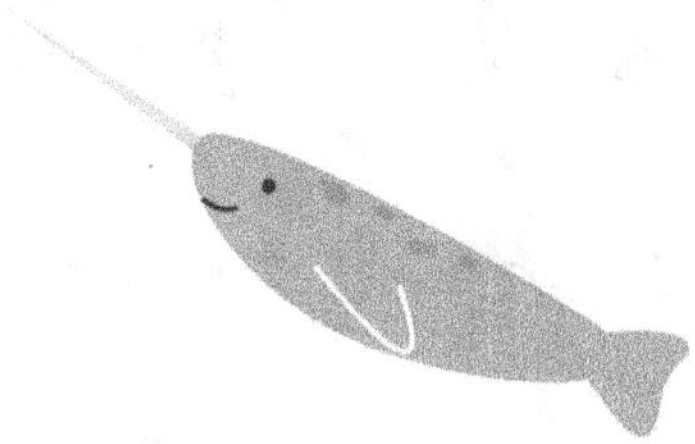

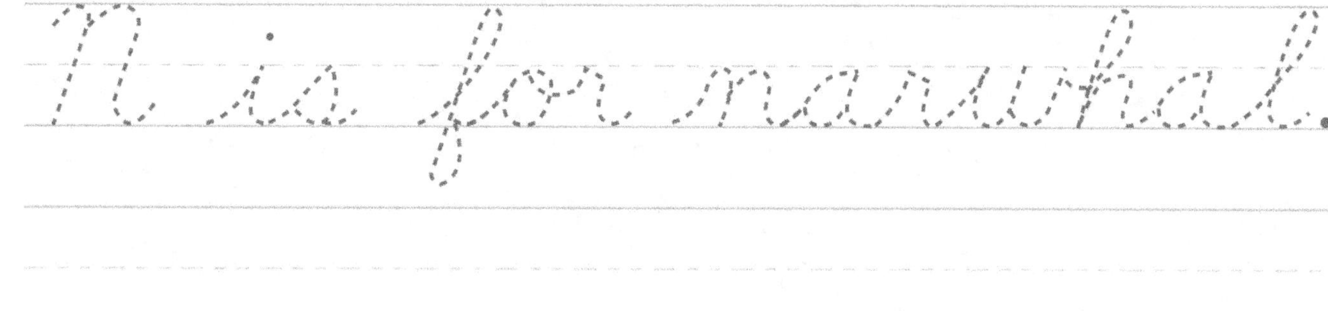

Trace the cursive letters, then write your own.

N N N

N N N

n n n

n n n

Trace the sentence written in script, then write your own.

N is for narwhal.

# O is for Octopus

Trace the cursive letters, then write your own.

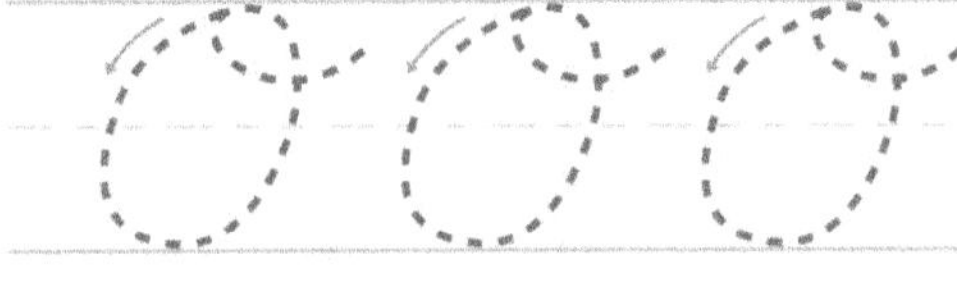

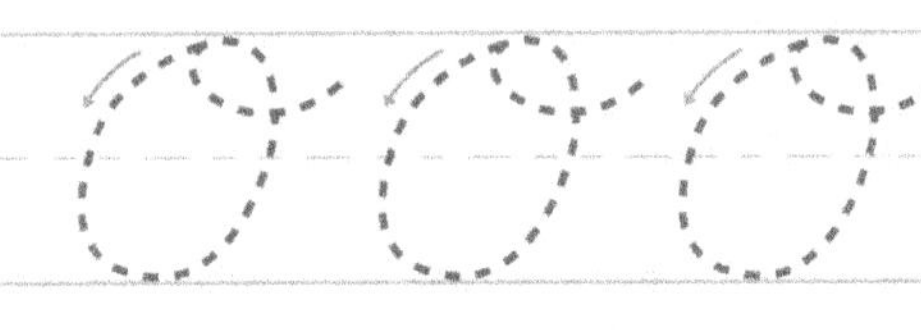

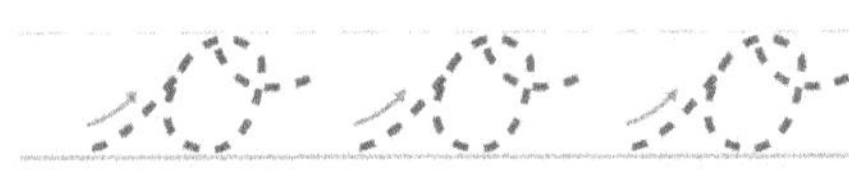

Trace the sentence written in script, then write your own.

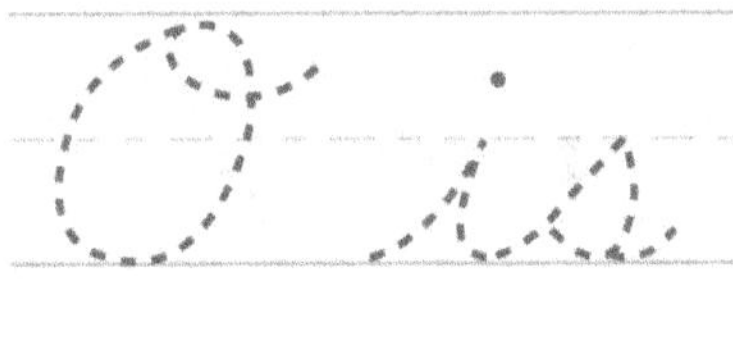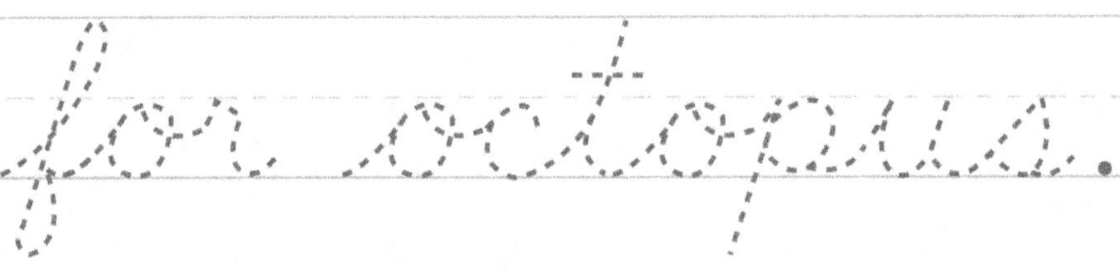

# P is for Penguin

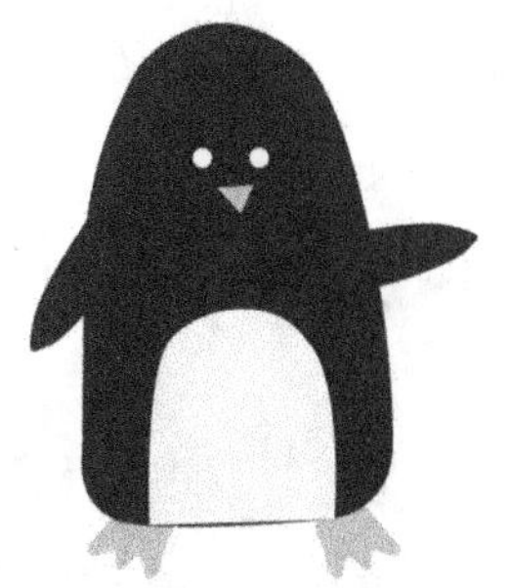

Trace the cursive letters, then write your own.

P P P

P P P

p p p

p p p

Trace the sentence written in script, then write your own.

P is for penguin.

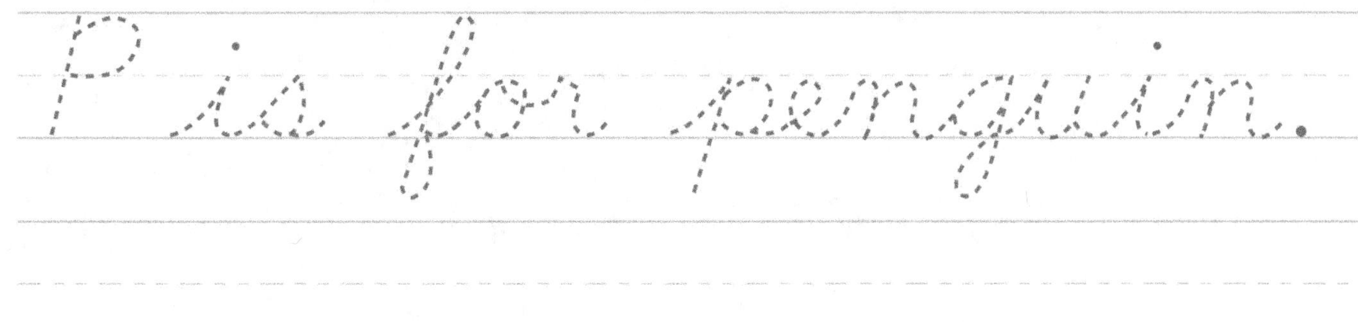

# Q is for Quail

Trace the cursive letters, then write your own.

Trace the sentence written in script, then write your own.

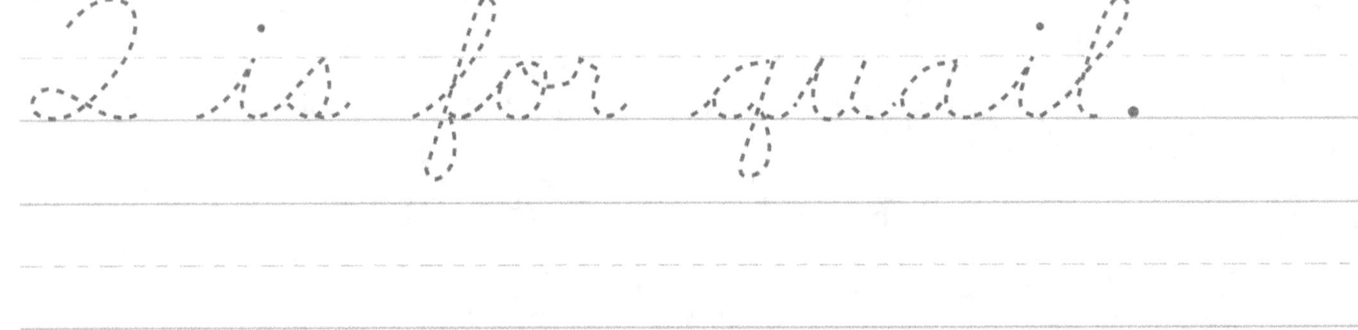

# R is for Rabbit

Trace the cursive letters, then write your own.

Trace the sentence written in script, then write your own.

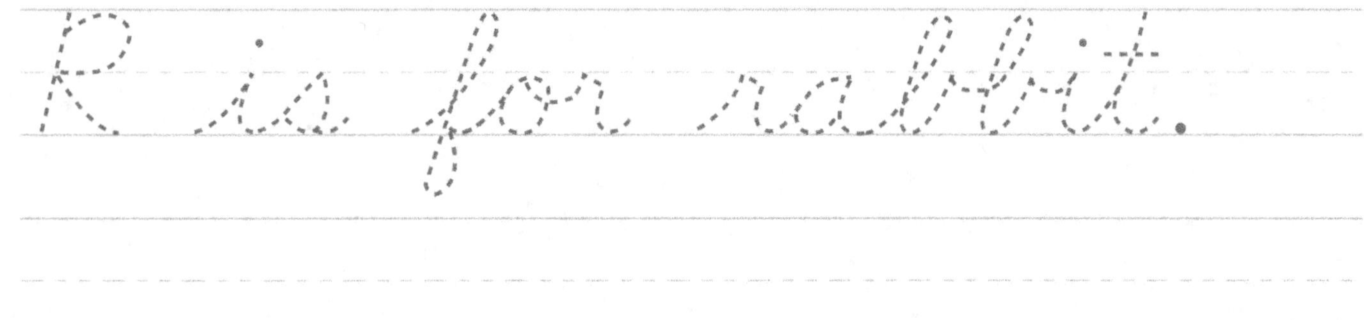

# S is for Squirrel

Trace the cursive letters, then write your own.

Trace the sentence written in script, then write your own.

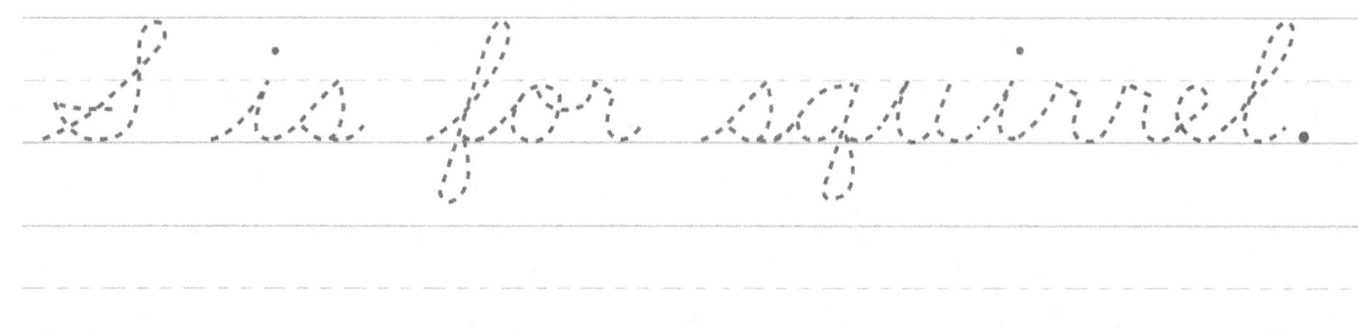

# T is for Turtle

Trace the cursive letters, then write your own.

Trace the sentence written in script, then write your own.

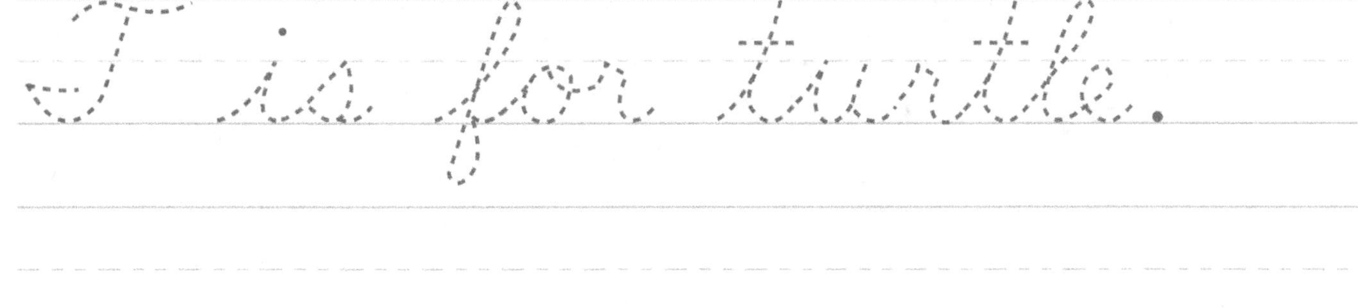

# U is for Urchin

Trace the cursive letters, then write your own.

Trace the sentence written in script, then write your own.

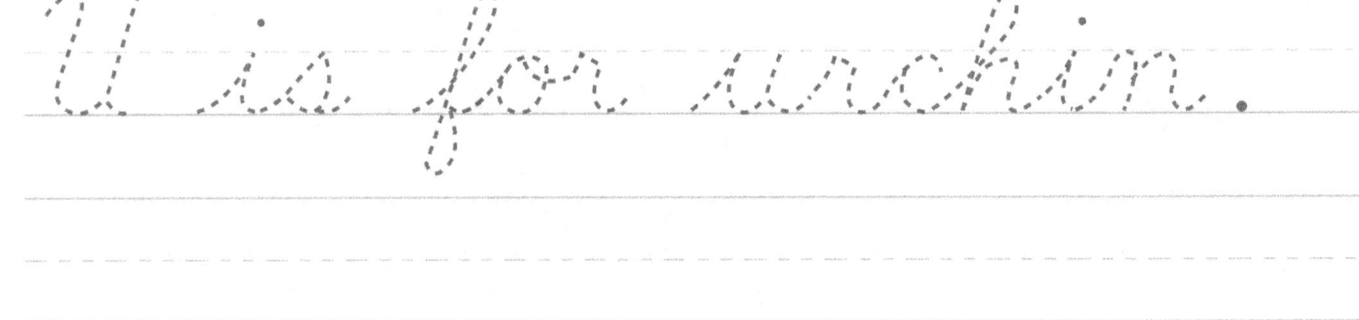

# V is for Vulture

Trace the cursive letters, then write your own.

Trace the sentence written in script, then write your own.

# W is for Whale

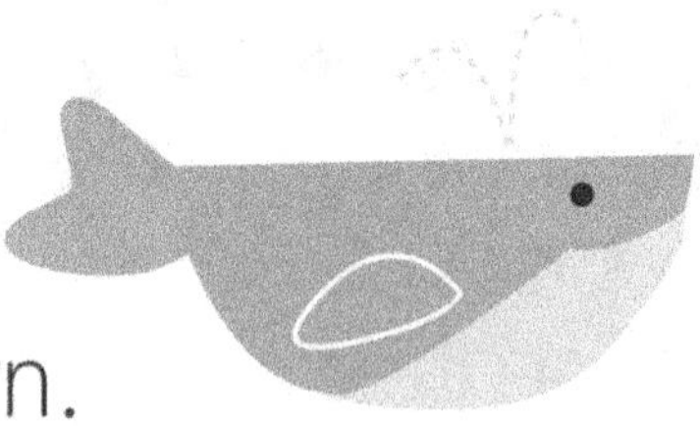

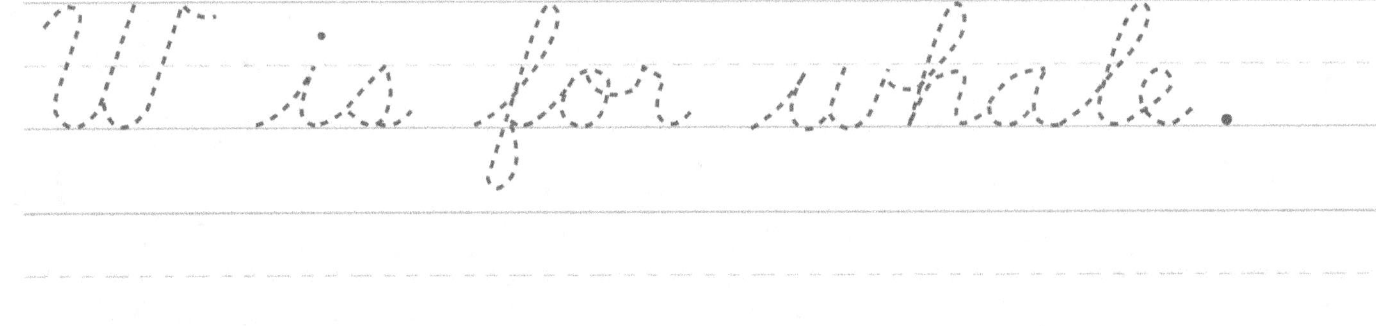

Trace the cursive letters, then write your own.

W W W

W W W

w w w

w w w

Trace the sentence written in script, then write your own.

W is for whale.

# X is for X-Ray Fish

Trace the cursive letters, then write your own.

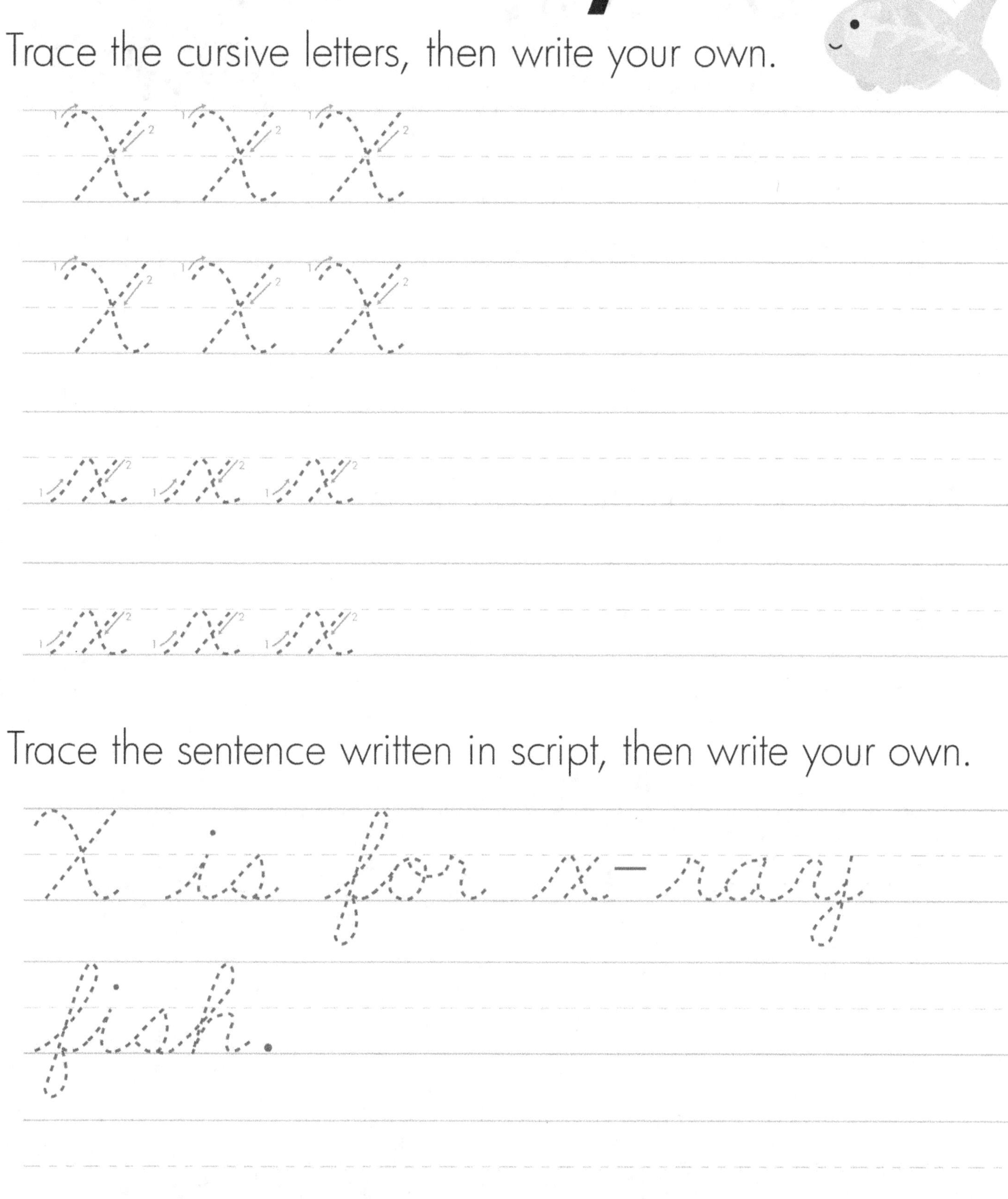

Trace the sentence written in script, then write your own.

# Y is for Yak

Trace the cursive letters, then write your own.

Trace the sentence written in script, then write your own.

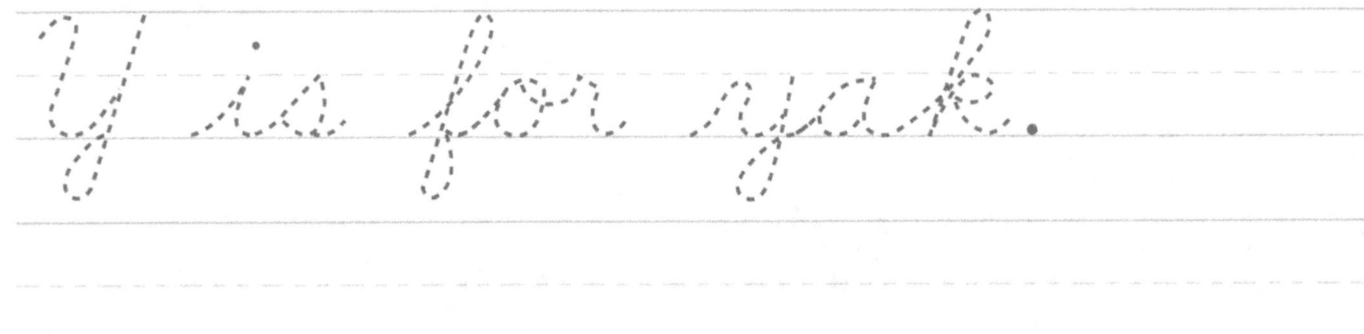

# Z is for Zebra

Trace the cursive letters, then write your own.

Trace the sentence written in script, then write your own.

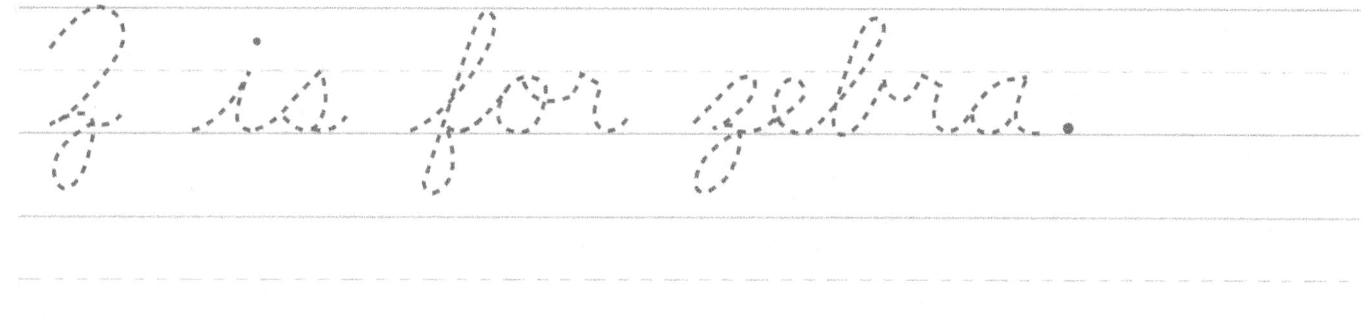

# My Name Is

Write your first name in cursive three times on the lines.

Write your last name in cursive three times on the lines.

# My Family

In cursive, write the names of:

Your parent(s):

Your sibling(s):

Your pet(s):

Let's practice punctuation with these extremely helpful worksheets.

# Capitals in Titles

## Capitalization Reminders for Titles:
- The first and last words are capitalized
- Nouns, verbs, adjectives, and adverbs are capitalized
- Specific names (such as the name of a person) are capitalized

Look at the title in each row.  Find the letters that need to be capitalized.  Rewrite the title that includes the correct capital letters in the space next to each title. The first example is done for you.

| | Title | Corrected Title |
|---|---|---|
| | the great bunny chase | The Great Bunny Chase |
| 1 | inspector hopper goes missing | |
| 2 | birds of the jungle | |
| 3 | the mystery of the missing key | |
| 4 | a tea party to remember | |
| 5 | schools around the world | |
| 6 | amy's rollercoaster adventure | |
| 7 | flowers for frances | |
| 8 | tiniest animals of the world | |
| 9 | explorations of outer space | |
| 10 | the new neighbors | |

# Punctuation: Commas

Insert commas in the sentences below.
Remember that commas are needed when:
1) Listing a series: I ate a hot dog, ice cream,  a burger and soda.
2) Before conjunctions: I slept all summer, but still felt accomplished.
3) Before parentheses: "I don't want summer to end," Kyle sighed.
4) After introductory elements: As a child, my favorite part of  summer
   was not having to go to school.

1.  This summer I am going to read play with friends and go to the beach.

2. Watermelon a refreshing fruit is nice to eat on a hot day.

3. My ice cream which is chocolate flavored is melting fast.

4. I will miss my friends but I will enjoy the break from school.

5. The baseball game which started at 5 was the perfect way to spend a summer evening.

6. While we were at the market mom and dad bought food for the July 4th barbeque.

7. "I would like to invite you to my pool party" my friend Veronica said.

8. My brother grandma and aunt bought root beer floats.

9. Although I don't want to get sunburnt I like laying out on the grass.

10. Since we are expecting crowds at the boardwalk we plan to arrive early.

11.  Sunny Stroll the local pier is always a fun place to go during summer evenings.

12. I bought new shorts sunglasses swimsuits and tank tops for the summer weather.

13. Our summer reading list includes Maniac Magee A Wrinkle in Time and Tuck Everlasting.

14. I will be sad when summer ends but I look forward to the new school year.

# Commas in Dates and Addresses

| How to Format Commas in Dates | How to Format Commas in Addresses |
| --- | --- |
| • Use a comma to separate the day from the year.<br>• Add a comma after the year if it comes in the beginning or middle of a sentence.<br><br>On October 24, 1945, the United Nations was founded. | • Use a comma to separate the street address, city, state, and country.<br>• Add a comma if the end of the address comes in the beginning or middle of a sentence.<br><br>We visited the U.N. headquarters at 405 East 42nd Street, New York. |

**Instructions: Add commas where they belong in each sentence.**

1 The world's first artificial satellite Sputnick was launched on October 4 1957.

2. The play "Hamilton" first appeared on Broadway on February 17 2015.

3. The Empire State Building is located at 20 West 34th Street New York.

4. My mother was born on August 21 1980 in Beijing China.

5. The Golden Gate Bridge first opened on May 27 1937.

6. Artist Frida Kahlo was born on July 6 1907.

7. The class went on a field trip to the Bishop Museum in Honolulu Hawaii.

8. The artist Yayoi Kusama was born on March 22 1929 in Nagano Prefecture Japan.

9. My favorite ice cream shop is located at 4525 SE Woodstock Blvd Portland Oregon.

10. The American artist Kehinde Wiley grew up in Los Angeles California.

**Instructions: Answer the questions, then add commas where they belong in each sentence.**

1. When were you born? ______________________________________________

2. Where were you born? ______________________________________________

3. What is your address?______________________________________________

4. What is a date you will always remember? ______________________________

5. Where did your grandparents meet? (City and state.) ______________________

# Perfect Punctuation

Rewrite the paragraph, adding commas, periods and capital letters where needed.

our solar system includes the sun and all the planets moons dwarf planets and asteroids that orbit around it the four planets closest to the sun include mercury venus earth and mars these inner planets are made of rock and metals they are quite small compared to the outer planets the four outer planets are called gas giants because they are made mostly of gases  the outer planets include jupiter saturn uranus and neptune the most well-known dwarf planet in our solar system is pluto

_______________________________

_______________________________

_______________________________

_______________________________

_______________________________

_______________________________

_______________________________

_______________________________

_______________________________

_______________________________

Name_________________________________________ Date_______________

Use a **comma** before the conjunction in a **compound sentence**.

- - - - - - - - - - - - - - - - - - - - - - - - - - - - - - - - - - - - -

Combine the sentences into a compound sentence.

1. I like to visit the museum. I always take a camera with me.

   _I like to visit the museum, and I always take a camera with me._

2. I enjoy the dioramas showing sea life. My favorite room has a complete skeleton of a shark.

   _______________________________________________

   _______________________________________________

3. Animals from Africa are in another room. They are just models.

   _______________________________________________

   _______________________________________________

4. I went to the museum yesterday. There was a new exhibit.

   _______________________________________________

   _______________________________________________

5. I wanted to go in. It wasn't open yet.

   _______________________________________________

   _______________________________________________

6. Mom said we could go tomorrow. I plan to be first in line.

   _______________________________________________

   _______________________________________________

# Quotation Marks

with Punctuation Pig

Let's learn another way to use quotation marks! Quotation marks are used around words that are titles. A title can be the name of a book, TV show or movie. Here is an example:

My favorite story is called "The Three Little Pigs".

Now you try!  Add quotation marks where they are needed in the sentences below.

1. My favorite television show is Yellow Bird Street.

2. My big sister likes to watch the TV show Teen Dream.

3. Yesterday, my mom bought me a new Owl Guy comic!

4. On Saturday morning, I always watch Karate Birds.

5. Today we finished the story of Jack and The Pop Quiz.

6. My friend Emily lent me the movie Crazy Trucks.

7. I wrote a story called Ants in My Pants.

8. We watched the movie The Secret Inside My Lunchbox.

---

**Answer the questions below and don't forget to use quotation marks!**

1. What is your favorite movie?

2. What is your favorite cartoon?

3. What is the name of a story that you read?

4. Write the name of a comic book that you like.

5. What is your favorite fairytale?

# Initials and Abbreviations

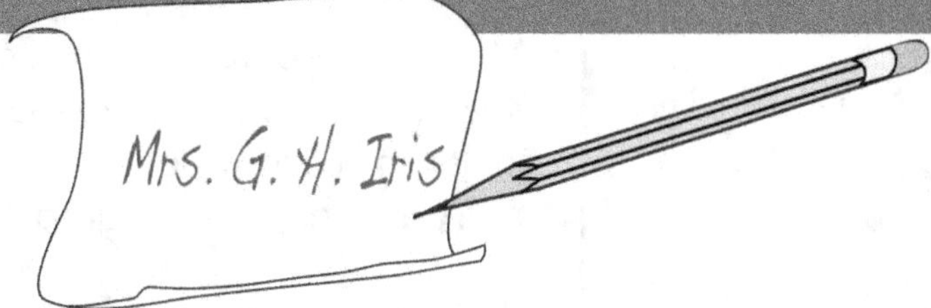


An *abbreviation* is a shorter form of a word or name. Use a period at the end of an abbreviation or after letters in a name.

*Remember:* If the word or name is capitalized, you should capitalize the abbreviation, too!

Write the correct abbreviations for the words below. If you need help, you can look them up in a dictionary!

1. Mister _______________
2. Missus _______________
3. January _______________
4. Tuesday _______________
5. Street _______________
6. Avenue _______________
7. Thursday _______________
8. Teaspoon _______________
9. Doctor _______________
10. Inch _______________
11. Junior _______________
12. Senior _______________

Use numbers or initials to write the correct abbreviations.

1. Aaron Byron Cane _______A. B. Cane_____________________
2. Doctor Dana Evelyn Frost _______________________________
3. The thirtieth of July _______________________________
4. Four feet, six inches _______________________________
5. 827 Eucalyptus Drive _______________________________
6. 46 Begonia Street _______________________________

# Quotation Marks

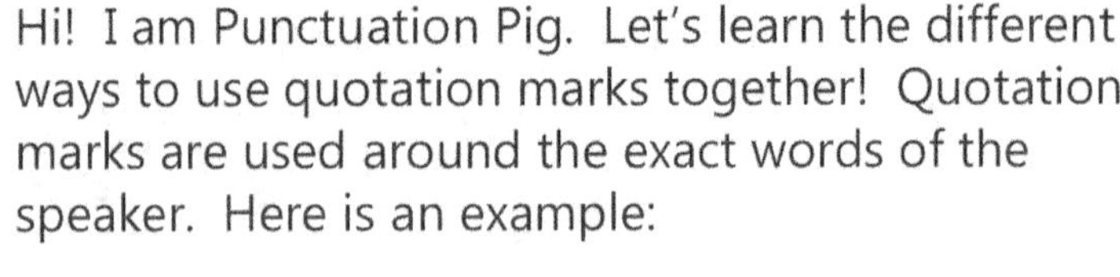


Hi! I am Punctuation Pig. Let's learn the different ways to use quotation marks together! Quotation marks are used around the exact words of the speaker. Here is an example:

"I will huff and I will puff and I will blow your house down!" said the wolf.

Now you try! Add quotation marks where they are needed in the sentences below.

1. What are we having for dinner? asked Emily.

2. We are having spaghetti, answered Mom.

3. Don't forget the meatballs, said Dad.

4. What are you doing on the weekend?  asked Chris.

5. My dad is taking me to the zoo!  said Sammy.

6. How did you do on your english test? Yannick asked.

7. I think I did well, Karyn answered.  How about you?

8. I got a ten on ten!  said Yannick with a smile.

9. What game do you want to play at recess?  Franco asked.

10.  Let's play hide and go seek, said Joey.

**Use the lines below to write your own story about a conversation between two friends.  Don't forget to use quotation marks!**

# Apostrophes in Possessives



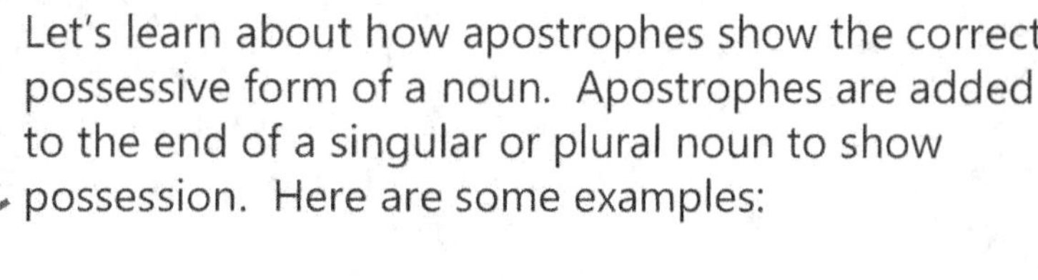


**Add apostrophes to show the correct possessive form of the nouns.**

1.  Emily s hands are cold because she has no gloves.
2.  Sammy went to buy his mother s birthday present.
3.  Mom s roast chicken and gravy was very yummy!
4.  Chris borrowed Yannick s ipod to listen to music on the way to his family s country house.
5.  The teacher s classroom was empty and silent.
6.  The tree s branches were covered with blooming flowers.
7.  Yannick s house is facing the Smith s house.
8. All the boy s uniforms were covered in grass stains after today s soccer game.

**Write a sentence using the correct possessive form of each noun.**

1. mermaid

2. ninjas

3. Officer Joe

4. Olsens

# Apostrophes in Contractions

**Add apostrophes in the sentences below.**

1. Laurie hopes she ll get a cat one day.

2. He s always playing video games!

3. Her mother hasn t gone grocery shopping yet.

4. We ll go to see a movie together tomorrow.

5. There s no milk left to dip my cookies in!

6. What if she d gone to bed earlier?  Maybe she wouldn t be so tired this morning.

7. Don t you think that horses are wonderful?

8. I m going to go home and watch cartoons.

**Write the contractions for the words below.**

1. there is

2. I am

3. you will

4. did not

5. have not

6. would have

7. I have

8. she is

9. they had

10.  there is

# Editing: Capitalization and Punctuation

*Use the COPS Editing strategy to make this student's writing better!  You should find **15 COPS mistakes**.  Then write the paragraph correctly on the lines.*

Capitalization: Did you capitalize the right words?
Organization: Did you organize the words in a complete sentence?  Did you indent at the beginning of a paragraph?
Punctuation: Did you use correct punctuation?
Spelling: Did you use correct spelling?

---

### Editing Marks

| | | | |
|---|---|---|---|
| ≡ Capitalize letter | | ✄ Take words or letters out | |
| ⊙ Add a period | | ◯ Correct spelling | |
| ? Add a question mark | | / Lowercase letter | |
| ∧ Add a word or comma | | ¶ Indent | |

---

have you ever been to new york city  my trip over happened the summer and it

was awesome.  We saw the statue of liberty and Ellis Island one day.  My parents

took my sister and me to a Broadway show, witch was really cool.  My favorite

part was when we road the trains and saw tall and buildings

___________________________________________

___________________________________________

___________________________________________

___________________________________________

___________________________________________

___________________________________________

# Edit to Improve It

*This student needs help with her writing!  She has mistakes in her writing.  Use the symbols from the Editing Marks box to fix the sentences.  Then write them correctly on the lines.*

---

### Editing Marks

| | | | |
|---|---|---|---|
| ≡ | Capitalize letter | ✋ | Take words or letters out |
| ⊙ | Add a period | ◯ | Correct spelling |
| ? | Add a question mark | / | Lowercase letter |
| ∧ | Add a word or comma | ¶ | Indent |

---

**1.** moving day was really

_______________________________________

_______________________________________

**2.** I found myself laughing, crying, and being silly all at the same time i didn't even know what to feel.

_______________________________________

_______________________________________

**3.** my best friend came over to say.

_______________________________________

_______________________________________

**4.** The truck was packed and ready to go we drove away slowly and waved goodbye

_______________________________________

_______________________________________

**5.** I felt much better when we got on the road my family started telling jokes.

_______________________________________

_______________________________________

# Editing: Capitalization, Punctuation, and Spelling

*This student needs help fixing her paragraph.  Use the Editing Marks below to make corrections to her work.  You should find **nine capitalization, punctuation, and spelling mistakes**.  Then, rewrite the paragraph correctly on the lines.*

## Editing Marks

| | | | |
|---|---|---|---|
| ≡ | Capitalize letter | ✍ | Take words or letters out |
| ⊙ | Add a period | ◯ | Correct spelling |
| ? | Add a question mark | / | Lowercase letter |
| ∧ | Add a word or comma | ¶ | Indent |

the day i got my dog was the best day of my life  I knew right away that

my dog and I would be best frends.  i chose the name Coach for him.  Its the

perfect name for him becaus when my dad and i throw the ball around

outside, coach barks.  It's like he is a baseball coach yelling from the dugout!

________________________________________

________________________________________

________________________________________

________________________________________

________________________________________

________________________________________

# Sentence Stretching

Prepositions and prepositional phrases can be used to give more information about our topic. Our sentences can be longer and more specific!

Use prepositions from the word bank to extend the sentences below and provide more details. Write each new sentence on the matching line. Look at the example below to get started.

### Word Bank

| before | above | toward |
|--------|-------|--------|
| onto | during | between |

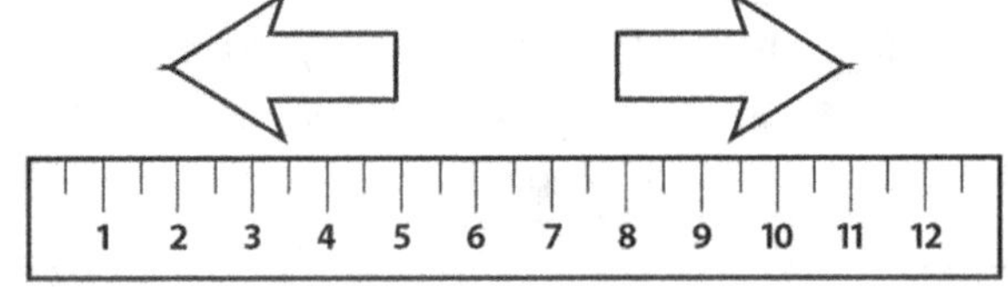

### Example:

Starting Sentence:  Scott sat in the car.

New Sentence:  Scott sat between his two sisters throughout the long car ride.

1. Starting Sentence:  Lacey's dog jumped.

   New Sentence: _______________________________________________

   _______________________________________________

2. Starting Sentence:  Look in the cabinet.

   New Sentence: _______________________________________________

   _______________________________________________

3. Starting Sentence:  On the screen I saw an announcement that you shouldn't talk.

   New Sentence: _______________________________________________

   _______________________________________________

4. Starting Sentence:  It is important to buy the airplane tickets.

   New Sentence: _______________________________________________

   _______________________________________________

5. Starting Sentence:  Jessie ran.

   New Sentence: _______________________________________________

   _______________________________________________

# Hey Neighbor!

Complete each word with **ie** or **ei**.

Remember, **i** usually comes before **e**, except:
- when it comes after **c** as in c**ei**ling
- when **e** and **i** make a **long a** sound as in fr**ei**ght

Another word for "get" is "rec __ __ ve."

A person who steals is a th __ __ f.

The knight carries a sword and a sh __ __ ld.

When you step on a scale, you can see your w __ __ ght.

Your pal is also your fr __ __ nd.

Santa rides on a red sl __ __ gh.

The opposite of floor is c __ __ ling.

The ch __ __ f is the leader.

You should be qu __ __ t in the library.

The number after seven is __ __ ght.

The al __ __ n is not from planet Earth.

# Elaborating on Feelings

Strong feelings and details are connected!  As you consider each feeling or emotion below, add some details that could be related to that feeling.  The first example is done for you.

Read each emotion or feeling below.  Write an example of when you've experienced that feeling.

| Feeling or Emotion | I felt this way when... |
| --- | --- |
| Excited | Mom told us that we were going on a special vacation! |
| Scared | |
| Nervous | |
| Sad | |
| Upset | |
| Surprised | |
| Bored | |
| Restless | |
| Confused | |
| Tired | |
| Embarrassed | |

# Make it Realistic!

Read each excerpt that is imaginary.  Think about how you can write a new, realistic sentence and then write your sentence on the line.  The first one is done for you.

**Example:**
As Jessica played a game at recess, her arms stretched out and she tagged all twenty children at the same time!
Realistic Sentence: Jessica raced across the playground and tagged two students at the same time!

1. One by one, Mark ate thirty tacos in a single meal and said that he was still hungry!

   Realistic Sentence: _________________________________________________________

   _____________________________________________________________________________

2. Evangeline decided that she wanted to become an author.  By the end of the week, she had written and published five books that were bestsellers in the book  store.

   Realistic Sentence: _________________________________________________________

   _____________________________________________________________________________

3. As Marley hissed furiously, fire came out of his mouth and set the box on fire.

   Realistic Sentence: _________________________________________________________

   _____________________________________________________________________________

4. Mandy's cat jumped out of the tree and flew across town, landing on top of a building.

   Realistic Sentence: _________________________________________________________

   _____________________________________________________________________________

5. As I gazed into the backyard, I was amazed to see money growing on the bushes around the house.

   Realistic Sentence: _________________________________________________________

   _____________________________________________________________________________

# Write with Personality!

## These worksheets focus on personification, metaphors, and sensory language.

Personification

Personification is the practice of giving human qualities to non-living things or animals in writing and in art. Give the following objects human-like qualities by using the provided objects and keywords in a sentence. (Hint: Use the illustrations as a guide.)

example:

Personify the object using the provided keyword.

The book laughed as the girl tickled its pages.

book / laughed

sneakers / tired

STOP

stop sign / scolded

alarm clock / yelled

Great job!  On the back of this page, continue practicing what you have learned by personifying the objects below.

# airplane ▪ toaster ▪ chair

As a bonus activity, draw a picture of the sentence you create.

# Sensory Words

Good writers use sensory words which describe something according to one or more of the five senses: taste, smell, feel, sound and look.

Sort each sensory word according to the sense that it relates to.

BITTER    BRIGHT    BUZZING    CHATTERING    CLOUDY    FRUITY

FRAGRANT    SPARKLY    RADIANT    GOOEY    HUMMING    SALTY

SCENTED    SCRATCHY    STICKY    ROUGH    TANGY    STINKY    SWEET

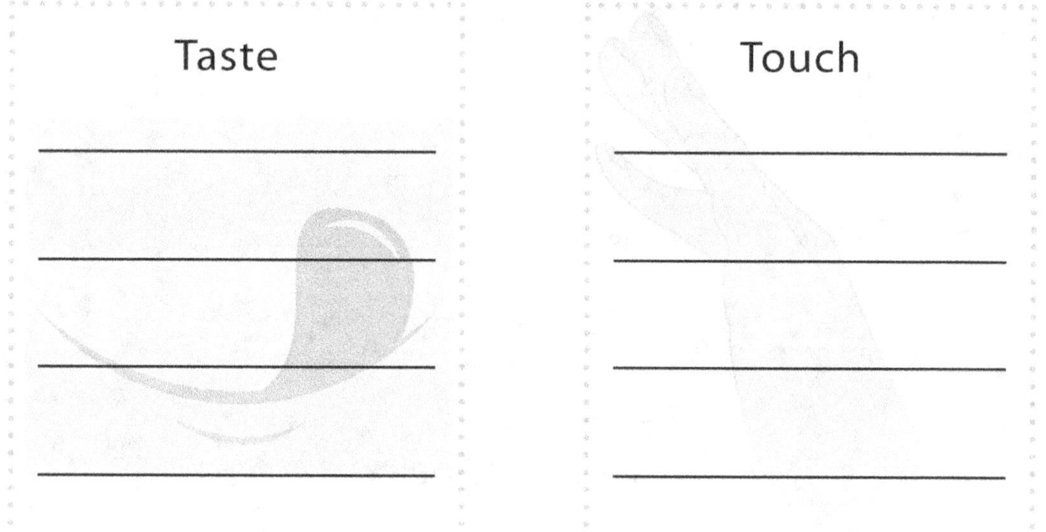

## Taste

__________________

__________________

__________________

__________________

## Touch

__________________

__________________

__________________

## Sight

__________________

__________________

__________________

__________________

## Sound

__________________

__________________

__________________

## Smell

__________________

__________________

__________________

# Clear as Crystal

Use the pictures as clues to complete each **simile**.

A **simile** is a phrase or figure of speech that compares two things using the words **like** or **as**.

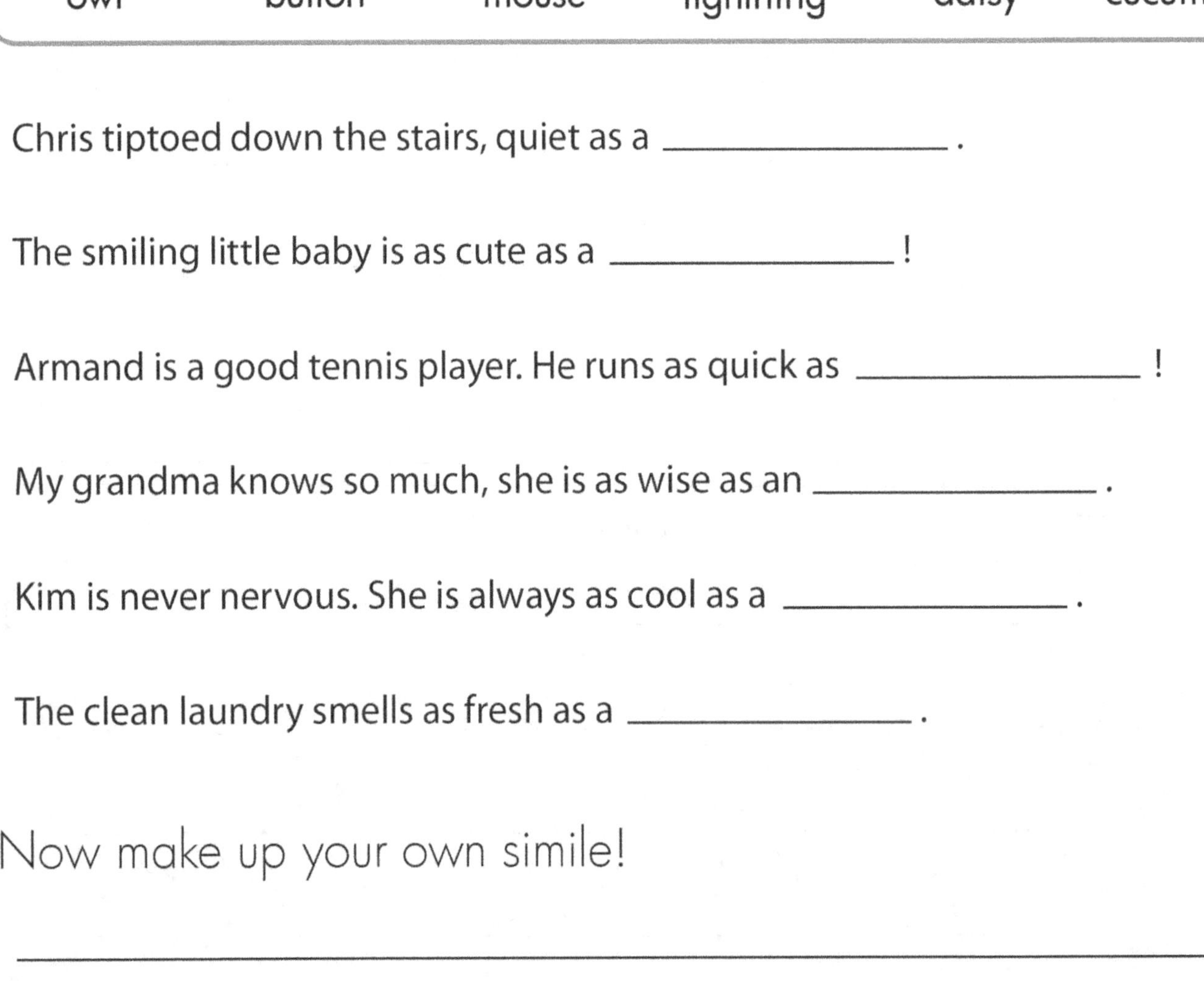



Chris tiptoed down the stairs, quiet as a ________________ .

The smiling little baby is as cute as a ________________ !

Armand is a good tennis player. He runs as quick as ________________ !

My grandma knows so much, she is as wise as an ________________ .

Kim is never nervous. She is always as cool as a ________________ .

The clean laundry smells as fresh as a ________________ .

Now make up your own simile!

________________________________________

________________________________________

# Cooking up Adjectives!

Sugar tastes **sweet** and is very **pleasant.** Spices taste **zesty** or **tangy.** Each spice is **unique** in flavor. Just as ingredients within a recipe determine how the food tastes, people have characteristics that describe how they act and what they are like. Words that define a person's personality are called **adjectives** (like **sweet, pleasant, tangy or unique**).

Below are recipe cards to list the adjectives that "make" your friends' and family's personalities. Choose a person based off of the adjective on the first line of each recipe, and then get creative by writing down more adjectives to describe each individual. Cutting lines are provided if you would like to cut up the recipes and share with those you choose to describe!

*Bona Appetite!*

Recipe for :

## Adventurous

Recipe for :

## Wise

Recipe for :

## Generous

Recipe for :

## Cheerful

# Make an Animal Metaphor!

Compare a car to a cheetah.  Or a person to a bee.
***My new car is a fast cheetah.  She is a busy bee.***
It's fun to think about these things.  On this page brainstorm a metaphor that
shows us how something or someone is like an animal.

| Animal | Person |
| --- | --- |
|  |  |

# Make an Animal Metaphor!

**Are you ready to turn your ideas into a poem?  Start simple.**
**Here is a suggestion for writing your first sentence:**

__________________________ is a(an) _______________________ .

(write the thing/person here)　　　　　　　　(write the animal here)

**In the lines below write some sentences to go along with your metaphor.**
**Turn this into a poem by making it rhyme or have a nice beat.**
**You'll be surprised at how clever this will sound.**

_____________________________________________

_____________________________________________

_____________________________________________

_____________________________________________

_____________________________________________

**Illustrate your metaphor!**

# My Animal Metaphor

A Poem By

Now that you understand metaphors, have fun creating more.
Write and illustrate your poem below.

# Graphic Organizer

Graphic organizers help writers generate ideas before they begin to write. Use the graphic organizer below to list sensory words that you might use if you were writing about a visit to an amusement park.

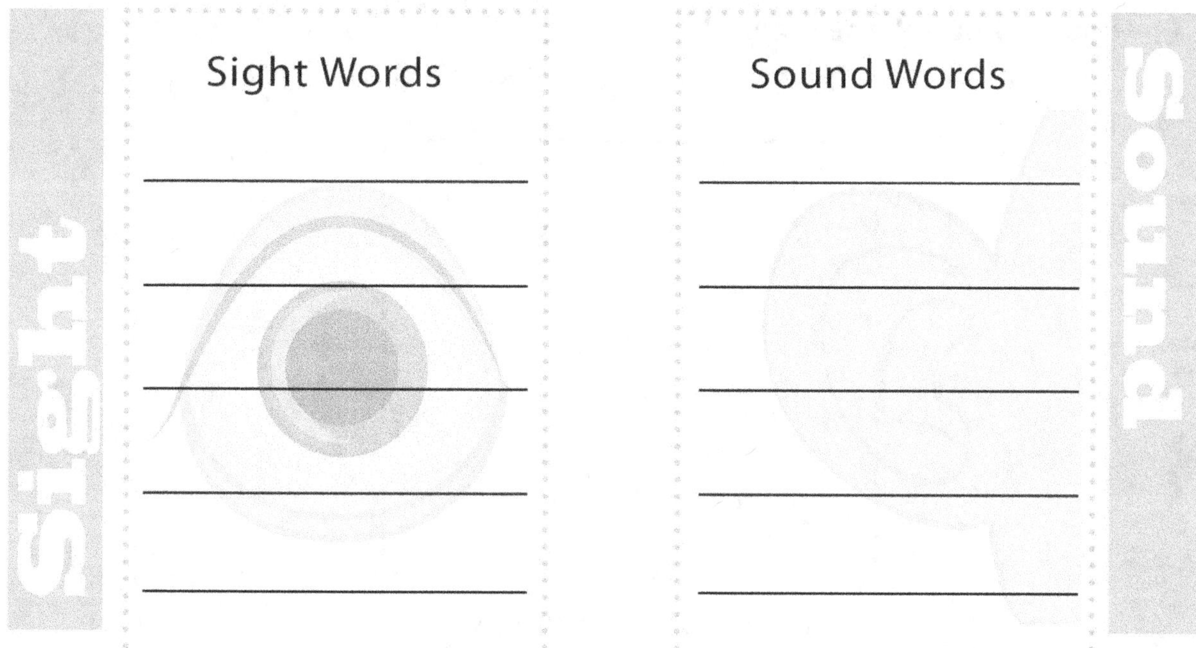

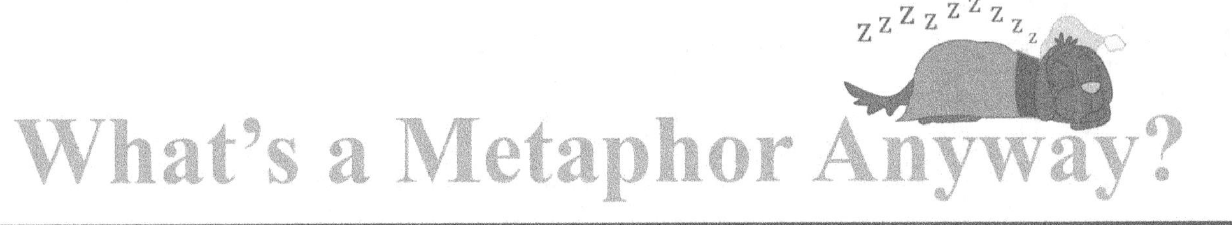

# What's a Metaphor Anyway?

Metaphor sounds like a big word, but you make metaphors all the time without even knowing it.
When you say something like, "I'm dog tired" or "I gobbled that all up," you are comparing yourself to
animals without really saying "Hey, I'm like a dog" OR "I'm like a goose."

**Poets do this all the time.  Read the poem by Carl Sandburg and
answer the questions to help you see the metaphor.**

# FOG

THE fog comes
on little cat feet.

It sits looking
over harbor and city
on silent haunches
and then moves on.

1. What is he comparing the fog to? _______________________________

2. List the words in the poem that make you think of this animal.

_______________________________________________

_______________________________________________

3. What does fog and this animal have in common?  How are they alike?

_______________________________________________

_______________________________________________

_______________________________________________

_______________________________________________

Improve your paragraph writing skills!
This set of worksheets focuses on organization and adding supporting details.
Flex those creative muscles, it's time to write!

# Story Order : Case 1

The entire class decided that the movie they watched was very exciting. First, a princess was kidnapped from her castle. Next, the main character magically became a knight in shining armor. Finally, the knight crossed the forest and saved the princess. Clearly, the movie was full of adventure.

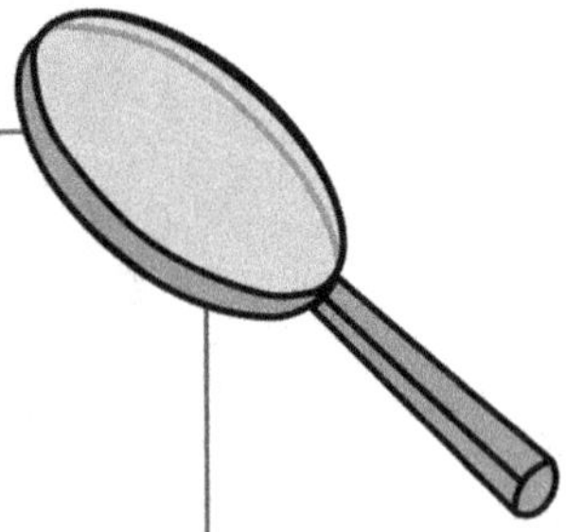

**Main Idea**

**Detail**

**Detail**

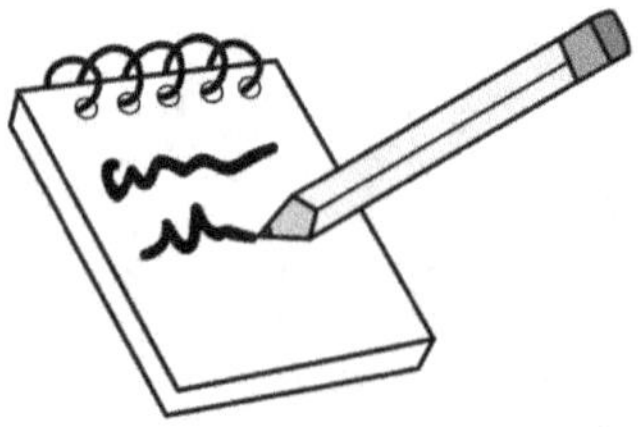

**Detail**

**Conclusion**

# Story Order : Case 2

Read the story, then write the main idea in the top box.
Next, summarize three details and a conclusion in the remaining boxes.

The Smith family would remember this vacation for a long time. They liked going camping, and first they got ready months ahead by going on hikes regularly. On their vacation they hiked down to the bottom of the Grand Canyon. Then they rafted down part of the Colorado River which runs through the canyon. Their river guide was knowledgeable and friendly. And, everyone had a good sense of humor. All these things came together to make for a memorable trip.

Main Idea

Detail

Detail

Detail

Conclusion

# Your Pet

## Supporting Details

**The Main Idea:** The most important idea in a paragraph.

**Supporting Details:** Details that tell you more about the main idea.

Supporting details make your main idea stronger!

**SUPPORTING DETAILS**

How long have you had your pet?

**SUPPORTING DETAILS**

What is your pet's name?

## MAIN IDEA

What kind of pet do you have?

**SUPPORTING DETAILS**

Describe your pet's personality?
Playful, loving, quiet, funny, loyal?

**SUPPORTING DETAILS**

What does your pet look like?
Describe your pet.

# Best Friends

## Supporting Details

**Supporting Details:** Details that tell you more about the main idea.

Supporting details make your main idea stronger!

**SUPPORTING DETAILS**

What do you do together?
What are your favorite activities?

**SUPPORTING DETAILS**

What does your best friend look like?

**MAIN IDEA**

Who is your best friend?
Why are you best friends?

**SUPPORTING DETAILS**

How long have you known
each other?

**SUPPORTING DETAILS**

What is your best friend like?
Describe his or her personality.

# Bubble Story Organizer

supporting details
topic

# Writing a Paragaraph

Choose one of the topics and fill in the graphic organizer by writing a topic sentence and three supporting details.

Topics:     Jungle          School          4th of July

Topic Sentence: ___________________________________

_______________________________________________________

Detail #1: _______________________________________________

_______________________________________________________

Detail #2: _______________________________________________

_______________________________________________________

Detail #3: _______________________________________________

_______________________________________________________

Write a complete paragraph using the topic sentence and details you wrote above.

_______________________________________________________

_______________________________________________________

_______________________________________________________

_______________________________________________________

# LADDER ORGANIZER

MAIN IDEA

SUPPORTING DETAIL

SUPPORTING DETAIL

SUPPORTING DETAIL

SUPPORTING DETAIL

SUPPORTING DETAIL

# Writing a Paragraph

Choose one of the topics and fill in the graphic organizer by writing a topic sentence and three supporting details.

Topics:     **Movies**        **Summer**        **Mini Golf**

Topic Sentence: ___________________________________

___________________________________________________

Detail #1: ________________________________________

___________________________________________________

Detail #2: ________________________________________

___________________________________________________

Detail #3: ________________________________________

___________________________________________________

Write a complete paragraph using the topic sentence and details you have provided above.

___________________________________________________

___________________________________________________

___________________________________________________

___________________________________________________

# SUPER HERO
## Supporting Details

**The Main Idea:** The most important idea in a paragraph.

**Supporting Details:** Details that tell you more about the main idea.

Supporting details make your main idea stronger!

**SUPPORTING DETAILS**
What are you like when you're not a hero? Are you an ordinary person? Do you hide out somewhere?

**SUPPORTING DETAILS**
What do you look like? Do you have a costume?

**MAIN IDEA**
If you could be a super hero, what would you be?

**SUPPORTING DETAILS**
What do you do with your powers? How do you help people?

**SUPPORTING DETAILS**
What are your super powers? What can you do that is special?

# Your Home
## Supporting Details

**The Main Idea:** The most important idea in a paragraph.

**Supporting Details:** Details that tell you more about the main idea.

Supporting details make your main idea stronger!

**SUPPORTING DETAILS**

What is your neighborhood like?
Do you live in a city, small town,
suburb, or the country?

**SUPPORTING DETAILS**

Who lives with you? Parents?
Brothers and sisters? Anyone else?

**MAIN IDEA**

What kind of home do you live in?
A house? An apartment? Describe it.

**SUPPORTING DETAILS**

What is outside your home? Do you
have a patio, yard or a garden?

**SUPPORTING DETAILS**

What is your room like?
Do you share your room? Describe it.

# When I Grow Up

## Supporting Details

**The Main Idea:** The most important idea in a paragraph.

**Supporting Details:** Details that tell you more about the main idea.

Supporting details make your main idea stronger!

### SUPPORTING DETAILS

What will you wear for this occupation? What equipment will you need?

### SUPPORTING DETAILS

Why do you want to be in this profession?

## MAIN IDEA

What do you want to be when you grow up?

### SUPPORTING DETAILS

What will you be doing every day?

### SUPPORTING DETAILS

How will you train for this profession? College, trade school, self-taught?

# Now, What Seems to be the Problem?

Just like fictional stories, personal narratives involve some kind of a problem, or conflict. Personal narratives are filled with feelings and emotions that often change throughout the story.

Problems could relate to:

> a disagreement you had with someone
> an obstacle you faced
> the challenge of learning something new
> getting through a tough time in your life
> something unexpected happened

## Feelings and Emotions:

serious    happy    scared    furious    sad    annoyed

frustrated    thrilled    excited    hurt    unwelcome

anxious    determined    confused    surprised

confident    shocked    warm    safe    inspired

Use the space below to brainstorm some ideas from your own life. Try to think of an instance where you experienced each type of problem described above and describe it below. Then write two or three feelings or emotions you felt during each experience. You can use the ideas from the box to help you, or come up with your own.

1. Once, I had a disagreement with ________________________about

_________________________________________________________________

_________________________________________________________________

Feeling __________________ Feeling __________________ Feeling __________________

2. An obstacle I had to overcome was _______________________________________

_________________________________________________________________

_________________________________________________________________

Feeling __________________ Feeling __________________ Feeling __________________

3. Even though it was really challenging, I finally learned how to __________________

_________________________________________________________________

_________________________________________________________________

Feeling __________________ Feeling __________________ Feeling __________________

4. I once had an unexpected ________________________________________________

_________________________________________________________________

_________________________________________________________________

Feeling __________________ Feeling __________________ Feeling __________________

5. I went through a tough time in my life when ___________________________

_______________________________________________________________________

_______________________________________________________________________

Feeling _________________  Feeling _________________  Feeling _________________


6. Once, I helped my _________________ deal with _________________

_______________________________________________________________________

_______________________________________________________________________

Feeling _________________  Feeling _________________  Feeling _________________


7. I was really surprised when _________________

_______________________________________________________________________

_______________________________________________________________________

Feeling _________________  Feeling _________________  Feeling _________________


8. I once failed at _________________ but then learned _________________

_______________________________________________________________________

_______________________________________________________________________

Feeling _________________  Feeling _________________  Feeling _________________


9. There was a time when I had to learn _________________

_______________________________________________________________________

_______________________________________________________________________

Feeling _________________  Feeling _________________  Feeling _________________

# TIME TO WRITE

Using the Story Map from the previous page, write your personal narrative from beginning to end. Begin your story in the moment that the experience began in your life, imagining you are looking at the experience through a microscope and describing every detail as it happened. Describe the problem, action, and the feelings you had from moment to moment, so your readers can create a movie of your experience in their minds as they read your narrative. Describe what you were thinking about during the experience and how the experience ended.

Title: _______________________________________________

## What is your favorite song? Write down the lyrics here.

**TITLE**

**LYRICS**

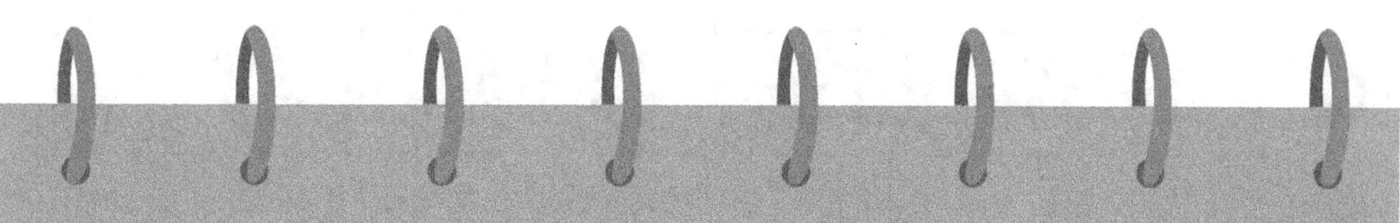

READ THE LYRICS AS IF THEY WERE A POEM.
WHAT DOES THIS SONG MEAN TO YOU?
DO YOU THINK THAT'S WHAT THE ARTIST INTENDED TO MEAN?

# Writing an Opinion

**Name** _______________________________     **Date** _______________

Think about something you would like to see changed in your school or class. Use the graphic organizer below to organize your ideas.

**1.** State your opinion. (What would you like to see changed?)

_______________________________________________

_______________________________________________

_______________________________________________

_______________________________________________

**2.** Describe the change in detail. (How would things change?)

_______________________________________________

_______________________________________________

_______________________________________________

_______________________________________________

**3.** Describe the benefits of your suggestion.
(Why should this change be made?)

_______________________________________________

_______________________________________________

_______________________________________________

Write a letter to your future self. This letter will be delivered to yourself in 10 years' time. What kinds of things do you hope to have accomplished by then? What things are important to you know? Are there any important current events that are going on right now? When you're finished, give your letter to your parents to save for you.

*Dear* _________________,

*Love,*

# First Person Narrative

First person narrative is a narrative mode where a story is narrated by one character at a time, speaking for and about themselves. First person narrative may be singular, plural, or multiple, and represents the point of view in the writing.

"I" is used to talk about yourself. "I" is always singular. "We" is used to talk about a group in which "I" is a member. "We" is plural.

**Examples:**

"I want to go shopping."  "We're hungry!"
"We thought he was joking."  "I wonder where she is."

**Directions:** Use your knowledge of first person narrative to write 10 original sentences in first person narrative.

**Sentences:**

1. _______________________________________________

2. _______________________________________________

3. _______________________________________________

4. _______________________________________________

5. _______________________________________________

6. _______________________________________________

7. _______________________________________________

8. _______________________________________________

9. _______________________________________________

10. _______________________________________________

# Writing Reviews

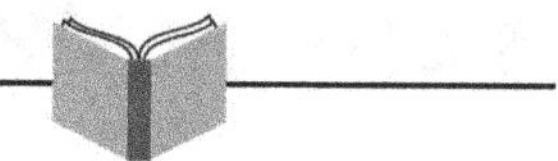

When you write a book report, you'll need to give an **opinion**. An opinion is the way you feel about something. For instance, you have an opinion on broccoli: you either like it or you don't like it. When professional writers give their opinion on a book, it's called a *review*.

However, when you're writing your report, you'll need to explain why you liked or didn't like your book! Start by writing a review of something you know well: a movie, a video game or a song. Write the details and information about it on the lines below.

Title: ___________________________________________________

Who made it? ___________________________________________

What happens in it? ______________________________________

_________________________________________________________

What do you like about it? _________________________________

_________________________________________________________

_________________________________________________________

What don't you like about it? ______________________________

_________________________________________________________

_________________________________________________________

Would you recommend it to a friend? ________________________

Why? ____________________________________________________

_________________________________________________________

# Write a Letter!

**Using the spaces below, write a letter to a friend or family member.**

Date ______________________

Dear __________________ ,

    What do you want to do on your next summer vacation? I would like to ______________________

______________________________________________

______________________________________________

______________________________________________

Then, ___________________________________

______________________________________________

______________________________________________

______________________________________________

Finally, _________________________________

______________________________________________

______________________________________________

______________________________________________

Please write back and tell me what you would like to do!

Sincerely,

______________________________

# Construct a Friendly Letter

Use the prompts and hints below to help you plan to write a friendly letter. Once you have organized your ideas on this page, use a separate piece of paper to write your friendly letter.

_______________________________

_______________________________

_______________________________

Hint: In these spaces, write your address and the date below your address. You can use your address or your school's address. Don't forget to use commas!

Dear _______________________________

Hint: Write the name of the person who is receiving your letter. Don't forget a comma!

Hint: In this space, write the body of the letter.

_______________________________________________________

_______________________________________________________

_______________________________________________________

_______________________________________________________

_______________________________________________________

_______________________________

End your letter with a closing, such as "Sincerely." Don't forget your comma!

_______________________________

Sign your name at bottom. You are finished!